DIABETIC *Air fryer* COOKBOOK

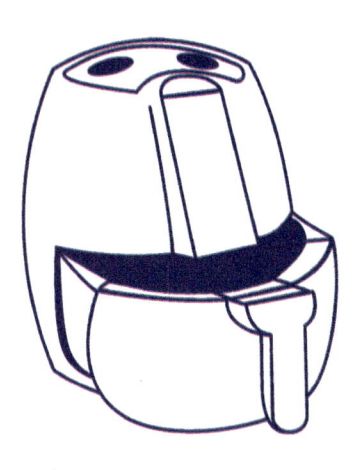

GEORGE PURTON

Copyright © 2024 George Purton. All rights reserved. No part of this book may be reproduced, distributed, or transmitted in any form or by any means, including photocopying, recording, or other electronic or mechanical methods, without the prior written permission of the publisher.

table of contents
REVIEW THE RECIPES IN THIS BOOK AT ONE GLANCE

Breakfast Recipes
- Nutty Granola with Yogurt
- Whole Grain Toast with Avocado and Poached Egg
- Bagel with Smoked Salmon and Cream Cheese
- Breakfast Stuffed Apples with Greek Yogurt
- Buckwheat Pancakes with Fresh Fruit
- Breakfast Quiche with Spinach and Goat Cheese
- Banana Bread with Walnuts
- Cauliflower and Egg Cups
- Breakfast Sausage and Egg Muffins
- Air-Fried Egg and Bacon Breakfast Pita

Appetisers and Sides
- Chicken Sausage and Bell Pepper Skewers
- Mini Cheese and Onion Pie
- Whole Grain Crispy Cheese and Spinach Rolls
- Mini Cornish Pasties with Cauliflower Crust
- Black Pudding and Apple Slices
- Welsh Rarebit Stuffed Portobello
- Fish Goujons
- Crispy Haggis Bites
- Mini Yorkshire Puddings with Roasted Zucchini
- Turkey Scotch Eggs

Poultry Recipes
- Chicken and Vegetable Pie
- Lemon Herb Chicken Thighs
- Chicken and Spinach Stuffed Peppers
- Tikka Skewers and Cauliflower Rice
- Broccoli Stuffed Chicken Breasts
- Honey Mustard Chicken Drumsticks
- Goose Breast with Rosemary and Garlic
- Goose Meatballs
- Turkey and Cranberry Stuffed Mushrooms
- Turkey and Apricot Meatloaf Minis

Beef Recipes
- Beef and Sweet Potato Pattie
- Beef Fajita Strips
- Meatballs with Zucchini Noodles
- Beef Koftas
- Beef and Cauliflower Tater Tot
- Welsh Beef and Swede Pasties
- Beef and Leek Cakes
- Beef and Pearl Barley Rissole
- Beef and Cabbage Rolls
- Welsh Rarebit Beef Burgers

Pork Recipes
- Stuffed Pork Loin with Spinach and Feta
- Pork Ribs with Sugar-Free BBQ Sauce
- Spiced Pork Collar Steaks
- Pork Cutlets with Almond Flour Breading
- Honey-Ginger Pork Tenderloin Skewers
- Garlic-Herb Pork Sirloin Roast
- Spicy Pork Sausage Patties
- Pork Ribeye Steaks with Mustard Glaze
- Belly Strips with Smoky Paprika Rub
- Pork Loin Chops with Herb Crust

Lamb Recipes
- Herb-Crusted Lamb Chops
- Rosemary Lamb Shoulder
- Lamb Koftas with Tzatziki Sauce:
- Tomato Zucchini Pasta with Lamb Meatballs
- Lamb Cutlets with Mint Pesto
- Lamb Shoulder Chops with Balsamic Glaze
- Garlic Lamb Shank with Mashed Cauliflower
- Lamb Eggplant Rolls
- Traditional Welsh Lamb Cawl
- Lamb Yogurt Sauce Sandwich

Fish Recipes
- Cod with Lemon and Herbs
- Haddock Fish and Chips
- Haddock with Spiced Cauliflower
- Salmon with Asparagus
- Mackerel with Lemon Dill Sauce
- Plaice with Almond Crust
- Mixed Fish Pie
- Cod and Cauliflower Fishcakes
- Mackerel with Roasted Vegetables
- Curried Cod

Other Seafood Recipes
- Mussels with Garlic and Herbs
- Basil and Tomato Mussels
- Lemon and Thyme Seasoned Cockles
- Crab Cakes
- Seafood Tacos
- Crab meat Sandwich
- Limpets with Herb Butter Shirataki Pasta
- Lemon Garlic Winkles with Zucchini Noodles
- Shrimp Scampi
- Crab Thermidor

Vegetarian Recipes
- Cauliflower Steaks
- Brussel Sprouts with Balsamic Glaze
- Asparagus with Lemon and Parmesan
- Chickpea Patties
- Sweet Potato and Black Bean Tacos
- Chestnut Mushroom Pie
- Portobello Mushroom Caps with Quinoa and Kale
- Cauliflower and Almond Fritters
- Zucchini and Lentil Stuffed Tomatoes
- Stuffed Eggplant with Quinoa and Spinach

Snacks
- Sweet Potato Skins
- Kale Chips
- Zucchini Fries
- Broccoli Tots
- Parmesan Eggplant Fries
- Courgette Fritters
- Cheesy Spinach Balls
- Chickpea Snacks
- Chicken Strips with Herbed Yogurt Dip
- Bacon-Wrapped Asparagus

Desserts
- Date and Almond Cake with Sugar-Free Toffee Sauce
- Almond Flour Chocolate Cupcake
- Sugar-Free Banana and Avocado Pie with Almond Crust
- Low-Carb Apple Crumble with Coconut Flour Crust
- Victoria Sponge Cake with Raspberry Chia Jam
- Treacle Tart with Almond Crust
- Lemon Chia Seed Cake with Stevia Glaze
- Scones with Sugar-Free Clotted Cream and Berry Compote
- Sugar-Free Bread and Butter Pudding with Coconut Cream

Diabetes and Nutrition

WELCOME TO THE KITCHEN, MATE!

In this cookbook dedicated to diabetes-friendly recipes, we're diving deep into delicious meals that won't mess with your blood sugar levels.

Now, let's talk about one of the most crucial aspects of managing diabetes: nutrition. We've got a whole section lined up just for this, where we introduce the nitty-gritty of diabetes and nutrition, helping you understand how food impacts your body and how to make smart, tasty choices every time you cook.

We'll explore the power of low glycemic foods and how they can be your best friend in keeping those blood sugar spikes at bay. From hearty whole grains to nutrient-packed veggies and lean proteins, we'll show you how to build balanced, satisfying meals that won't leave you feeling deprived.

Plus, we'll dish out tips on portion control, label reading, and making mindful swaps to transform your favourite dishes into diabetes-friendly delights.

Get ready to take control of your health one delicious bite at a time!

Behind Diabetes

KNOWING YOUR TYPE AND WHAT IT MEANS

Let's delve a but into the roots of diabetes type 1 and type 2.

Type 1 diabetes is like a bit of a mystery box – it's an autoimmune condition where your immune system mistakenly attacks and destroys the insulin-producing cells in your pancreas.

This means your body struggles to produce insulin, the hormone that helps regulate your blood sugar levels. It's often diagnosed in childhood or adolescence, and while the exact cause isn't fully understood, genetics and environmental factors seem to play a role.

Now, type 2 diabetes is a bit of a different kettle of fish. It's often linked to lifestyle factors, like being overweight or inactive. When you carry extra weight, especially around your middle, it can make your cells more resistant to insulin's effects.

This means your pancreas has to work harder to produce more insulin to keep your blood sugar in check. Over time, this can lead to insulin resistance and, eventually, type 2 diabetes.

But don't worry, mate, because with the right diet and lifestyle changes, you can take charge and manage your diabetes like a pro.

Diabetes 1 & 2 Nutrition

DOES MY TYPE MATTER?

There are some differences in the focus of nutritional needs between type 1 and type 2 diabetes

Type 1 diabetes requires a finely-tuned balance of carbs, as they directly affect blood sugar and insulin dosage. Type 2 diabetes focuses more on obesity management with calorie counting and portion sizes being an important tool to manage weight.

Despite these differences, both diabetes types share common ground when it comes to food. They thrive on a diverse array of nosh, with an emphasis on fruits, veggies, whole grains, lean proteins, and good fats. Keeping portions in check is crucial to both to avoid sugar spikes. And sticking to regular mealtimes helps maintain steady blood sugar levels throughout the day, boosting overall health.

In this cookbook, navigating these nutritional nuances will be as easy as pie (well, sugar-free pie!). Every recipe is meticulously crafted to provide detailed nutritional info, including carb content, protein, fats, sugars, sodium levels, and calorie counts. With clear guidance on portion sizes and the nutritional numbers you need, this cookbook sets you up with the smarts and scrumptiousness to make better choices for your health, whether you're managing type 1 or type 2 diabetes

Air Frying for Diabetes

MORE THAN A NIFTY GADGET

The airfryer–this popularized gadget is like your kitchen's best mate, especially for folks managing diabetes.

Why, you ask?

Well, air fryers use hot air circulation to cook food, cutting down on the need for excess oil. This means you can enjoy crispy delights without worrying about extra fats and calories. Plus, they're super versatile, whipping up everything from crunchy veggies to succulent meats in no time.

And here's the cherry on top: all the recipes in this cookbook are tailor-made for air fryer use. Yep, you read that right. That means no faffing about with complicated cooking methods or hours spent slaving over a hot stove.

With just a few simple steps and your trusty air fryer, you'll be whipping up delicious, diabetes-friendly meals quicker than you can say "fish and chips."

How to use this book

Short Guide on Utilising Information from the Cookbook

Before getting started, here's a quick rundown of how you'll get the best value out of this cookbook. You'll find all the essential info neatly laid out for you on each recipe page.

Nutrition Information
Let's start with the nutrition content section, where you'll see all the numbers that matter: carb content, protein, fats, sugars, sodium levels, and calorie counts. This gives you a clear picture of what you're putting on your plate and helps you make informed choices that fit your dietary needs.

Whole Grains, Healthy Fats, Lean Proteins
Next up, we highlight key recommended food and ingredients. If a recipe contains whole grains, healthy fats, or lean proteins, you'll see it marked with a * and we'll place a marker at the bottom of the page. Whole grains are packed with fibre and nutrients, while healthy fats like those from avocados or nuts are great for heart health. And let's not forget lean proteins, which are essential for muscle repair and overall well-being.

Portion Control
Portion control is another key aspect we focus on in this book. Each recipe specifies the exact amount of ingredients you need to prepare and use to make the healthy recommended portion for that food. Knowing exactly how much of which ingredient to put helps you manage your calorie intake and keeps your blood sugar levels steady. It's all about balance.

Create Your Meal Plan
Finally, when planning your meals, you can turn to our handy table of contents for the complete list of recipes. We've categorised them into food groups like poultry, beef, lamb, pork, fish, seashell (yep, we've got some sea-inspired dishes too!), and vegetables. This makes it easy to mix and match dishes, ensuring you get a variety of nutrients and flavours in your meals.

When you see these icons in red at the bottom of the page, we're letting you know that they've got key ingredients for diabetic health management!

Breakfast

Start your day on a high note with nutritious and delicious air fryer recipes tailored for diabetics.

Imagine tucking into a scrumptious air-fried granola bursting with flavour, or a crispy avocado toast that perfectly balances healthy fats and fibre. Don't forget the breakfast sausages and egg cups, giving you all the goodness without the grease. Dive into these recipes and make your mornings marvellous!

Nutty Granola with Yogurt

NUTRITION INFORMATION

- *Calories: 300*
- *Carbohydrates: 25g*
- *Protein: 10g*
- *Fats: 18g*
- *Sugar: 8g*
- *Sodium: 100mg*

DIRECTIONS:

1. In a bowl, mix rolled oats, chopped almonds, chopped walnuts, pumpkin seeds, sunflower seeds, coconut oil, honey or sugar-free sweetener, and cinnamon until well combined.
2. Spread the mixture evenly on the air fryer tray.
3. Air fry at 160°C (320°F) for 10-12 minutes, stirring halfway through cooking, until the granola is golden and crispy.
4. Let the granola cool completely before serving.
5. Serve with Greek yogurt and fresh berries.

* This recipe contains a healthy highlight that we don't recommend you switch with other ingredients

INGREDIENTS

- *1/2 cup rolled oats**
- *2 tablespoons chopped almonds*
- *2 tablespoons chopped walnuts*
- *1 tablespoon pumpkin seeds*
- *1 tablespoon sunflower seeds*
- *1 tablespoon coconut oil**
- *1 tablespoon honey or sugar-free sweetener*
- *1/4 teaspoon cinnamon*
- *1/4 cup Greek yogurt (unsweetened)*
- *Fresh berries for serving*

Using the measurements above will make exactly one serving of this meal. This serving size will match the nutritional information on this page.

Healthy Highlights:

- WHOLE GRAIN
- HEALTHY FATS
- LEAN PROTEIN

Toast with Avocado and Poached Egg

NUTRITION INFORMATION

- *Calories: 280*
- *Carbohydrates: 20g*
- *Protein: 12g*
- *Fats: 16g*
- *Sugar: 2g*
- *Sodium: 200mg*

DIRECTIONS:

1. Toast the whole grain bread for 10 minutes in the air fryer until crispy.
2. Spread the mashed avocado on top of the toast.
3. Poach the egg using your preferred method.
4. Place the poached egg on top of the avocado.
5. Season with salt and pepper to taste.
6. Serve immediately.

* This recipe contains a healthy highlight that we don't recommend you switch with other ingredients

INGREDIENTS

- *1 slice whole grain bread**
- *1/2 avocado*, mashed*
- *1 large egg*
- *Salt and pepper to taste*

Using the measurements above will make exactly one serving of this meal. This serving size will match the nutritional information on this page.

Healthy Highlights:

- WHOLE GRAIN
- HEALTHY FATS
- LEAN PROTEIN

11

Bagel with Smoked Salmon and Cream Cheese

NUTRITION INFORMATION

- Calories: 320
- Carbohydrates: 30g
- Protein: 15g
- Fats: 14g
- Sugar: 2g
- Sodium: 400mg

DIRECTIONS:

1. Slice the whole grain bagel in half and toast it in the air fryer for 10 minutes until lightly crispy.
2. Spread cream cheese on each half of the bagel.
3. Top one half with smoked salmon.
4. Garnish with fresh dill.
5. Sandwich the two halves together and serve.

INGREDIENTS

- 1 whole grain bagel*
- 2 tablespoons cream cheese (low-fat if preferred)
- 50g smoked salmon
- Fresh dill for garnish

Using the measurements above will make exactly one serving of this meal. This serving size will match the nutritional information on this page.

Healthy Highlights:

WHOLE GRAIN · HEALTHY FATS · LEAN PROTEIN

* This recipe contains a healthy highlight that we don't recommend you switch with other ingredients

Stuffed Apples with Greek Yogurt

NUTRITION INFORMATION

- *Calories: 250*
- *Carbohydrates: 30g*
- *Protein: 8g*
- *Fats: 10g*
- *Sugar: 15g*
- *Sodium: 50mg*

DIRECTIONS:

1. Core the apple, leaving the bottom intact to form a cup.
2. Mix granola, Greek yogurt, honey or sugar-free sweetener, and chopped nuts in a bowl.
3. Stuff the apple with the granola mixture.
4. Place the stuffed apple in the air fryer basket.
5. Air fry at 160°C (320°F) for 10-12 minutes until the apple is tender.
6. Serve warm as a delicious breakfast treat.

INGREDIENTS

- *1 large apple*
- *1/4 cup granola (sugar-free if possible)**
- *1/4 cup Greek yogurt (unsweetened)*
- *1 tablespoon honey or sugar-free sweetener*
- *1 tablespoon chopped nuts (such as almonds or walnuts)*

Using the measurements above will make exactly one serving of this meal. This serving size will match the nutritional information on this page.

Healthy Highlights:

WHOLE GRAIN · HEALTHY FATS · LEAN PROTEIN

* *This recipe contains a healthy highlight that we don't recommend you switch with other ingredients*

Buckwheat Pancakes with Fresh Fruit

NUTRITION INFORMATION

- *Calories: 280*
- *Carbohydrates: 30g*
- *Protein: 8g*
- *Fats: 14g*
- *Sugar: 8g*
- *Sodium: 300mg*

DIRECTIONS:

1. In a bowl, mix buckwheat flour, baking powder, and cinnamon.
2. Add the egg, almond milk, and melted coconut oil to the dry ingredients. Stir until well combined.
3. Preheat the air fryer to 180°C (356°F) for 3 minutes.
4. Lightly grease the air fryer basket with coconut oil.
5. Pour the pancake batter into the air fryer, spreading it evenly to form pancakes.
6. Cook for 4-5 minutes, then flip the pancakes and cook for an additional 2-3 minutes until golden brown and cooked through.
7. Serve the pancakes topped with fresh fruit.

* This recipe contains a healthy highlight that we don't recommend you switch with other ingredients

INGREDIENTS

- *1/2 cup buckwheat flour**
- *1/2 teaspoon baking powder*
- *1/4 teaspoon cinnamon*
- *1 egg*
- *1/4 cup unsweetened almond milk*
- *1 tablespoon coconut oil**
- *Fresh fruit for topping (such as berries, sliced banana)*

Using the measurements above will make exactly one serving of this meal. This serving size will match the nutritional information on this page.

Healthy Highlights:

- WHOLE GRAIN
- HEALTHY FATS
- LEAN PROTEIN

Breakfast Quiche with Spinach and Goat Cheese

NUTRITION INFORMATION

- Calories: 320
- Carbohydrates: 10g
- Protein: 15g
- Fats: 24g
- Sugar: 3g
- Sodium: 400mg

DIRECTIONS:

1. Preheat the air fryer to 180°C (356°F) for 3 minutes.
2. In a bowl, whisk together eggs, chopped spinach, crumbled goat cheese, salt, and pepper.
3. Grease a small oven-safe dish or ramekin with cooking spray or olive oil.
4. Pour the egg mixture into the greased dish.
5. Place the dish in the air fryer basket.
6. Cook for 10-12 minutes until the quiche is set and slightly golden on top.
7. Let the quiche cool slightly before serving.

*This recipe contains a healthy highlight that we don't recommend you switch with other ingredients

INGREDIENTS

- 2 eggs
- 1/4 cup chopped spinach
- 1/4 cup crumbled goat cheese
- Salt and pepper to taste
- Cooking spray or olive oil* (for greasing)

Using the measurements above will make exactly one serving of this meal. This serving size will match the nutritional information on this page.

Healthy Highlights:

WHOLE GRAIN — HEALTHY FATS — LEAN PROTEIN

Banana Bread with Walnuts

NUTRITION INFORMATION

- *Calories: 200*
- *Carbohydrates: 10g*
- *Protein: 15g*
- *Fats: 12g*
- *Sugar: 5g*
- *Sodium: 300mg*

DIRECTIONS:

1. Preheat the air fryer to 180°C (356°F) for 3 minutes.
2. In a bowl, mix grated cauliflower, eggs, chopped spring onions, grated cheese (if using), salt, and pepper.
3. Grease muffin cups or ramekins with cooking spray or olive oil.
4. Pour the cauliflower and egg mixture into the greased cups.
5. Place the cups in the air fryer basket.
6. Cook for 10-12 minutes until the egg cups are set and golden on top.
7. Let the egg cups cool slightly before serving.

INGREDIENTS

- *1 ripe banana, mashed*
- *1/4 cup almond flour**
- *1/4 cup oat flour**
- *1/4 cup chopped walnuts*
- *1 egg*
- *2 tablespoons honey or sugar-free sweetener*
- *1/4 teaspoon baking soda*
- *Pinch of salt*
- *Cooking spray or olive oil* (for greasing)*

Using the measurements above will make exactly one serving of this meal. This serving size will match the nutritional information on this page.

Healthy Highlights:

WHOLE GRAIN | HEALTHY FATS | LEAN PROTEIN

* This recipe contains a healthy highlight that we don't recommend you switch with other ingredients

Cauliflower and Egg Cups

NUTRITION INFORMATION

- *Calories: 200*
- *Carbohydrates: 10g*
- *Protein: 15g*
- *Fats: 12g*
- *Sugar: 5g*
- *Sodium: 300mg*

DIRECTIONS:

1. Preheat the air fryer to 180°C (356°F) for 3 minutes.
2. In a bowl, mix grated cauliflower, eggs, chopped spring onions, grated cheese (if using), salt, and pepper.
3. Grease muffin cups or ramekins with cooking spray or olive oil.
4. Pour the cauliflower and egg mixture into the greased cups.
5. Place the cups in the air fryer basket.
6. Cook for 10-12 minutes until the egg cups are set and golden on top.
7. Let the egg cups cool slightly before serving.

* This recipe contains a healthy highlight that we don't recommend you switch with other ingredients

INGREDIENTS

- *1/2 cup grated cauliflower*
- *2 eggs*
- *1 tablespoon chopped spring onions*
- *1 tablespoon grated cheese (optional)*
- *Salt and pepper to taste*
- *Cooking spray or olive oil* (for greasing)*

Using the measurements above will make exactly one serving of this meal. This serving size will match the nutritional information on this page.

Healthy Highlights:

WHOLE GRAIN | HEALTHY FATS | LEAN PROTEIN

Breakfast Sausage and Egg Muffins

NUTRITION INFORMATION

- *Calories: 250*
- *Carbohydrates: 5g*
- *Protein: 15g*
- *Fats: 18g*
- *Sugar: 2g*
- *Sodium: 350mg*

DIRECTIONS:

1. Preheat the air fryer to 180°C (356°F) for 3 minutes.
2. In a bowl, whisk eggs with chopped bell peppers, grated cheese (if using), salt, and pepper.
3. Grease muffin cups or ramekins with cooking spray or olive oil.
4. Divide the chopped breakfast sausages among the greased cups.
5. Pour the egg mixture over the sausages in each cup.
6. Place the cups in the air fryer basket.
7. Cook for 10-12 minutes until the egg muffins are set and golden on top.
8. Let the muffins cool slightly before serving.

INGREDIENTS

- *2 eggs*
- *2 breakfast sausages, cooked and chopped*
- *1 tablespoon chopped bell peppers*
- *1 tablespoon grated cheese (optional)*
- *Salt and pepper to taste*
- *Cooking spray or olive oil* (for greasing)*

Using the measurements above will make exactly one serving of this meal. This serving size will match the nutritional information on this page.

Healthy Highlights:

WHOLE GRAIN | HEALTHY FATS | LEAN PROTEIN

* This recipe contains a healthy highlight that we don't recommend you switch with other ingredients

Air-Fried Egg and Bacon Breakfast Pita

NUTRITION INFORMATION

- Calories: 300
- Carbohydrates: 25g
- Protein: 15g
- Fats: 15g
- Sugar: 2g
- Sodium: 400mg

DIRECTIONS:

1. Preheat the air fryer to 180°C (356°F) for 3 minutes.
2. Grease the air fryer basket with cooking spray or olive oil.
3. Place the whole grain pita in the basket and gently press down the centre to create a well.
4. Crack the egg into the well of the pita.
5. Sprinkle chopped bacon and grated cheese (if using) over the egg.
6. Season with salt and pepper.
7. Air fry for 5-6 minutes until the egg is cooked to your desired doneness and the pita is crispy.
8. Serve hot and enjoy your delicious breakfast pita.

* This recipe contains a healthy highlight that we don't recommend you switch with other ingredients

INGREDIENTS

- 1 whole grain pita*
- 1 egg
- 2 slices cooked bacon, chopped
- 1 tablespoon grated cheese (optional)
- Salt and pepper to taste
- Cooking spray or olive oil* (for greasing)

Using the measurements above will make exactly one serving of this meal. This serving size will match the nutritional information on this page.

Healthy Highlights:

- WHOLE GRAIN
- HEALTHY FATS
- LEAN PROTEIN

Appetisers and Sides

Elevate your meals with diabetic-friendly appetisers and sides made effortlessly in the air fryer.

Picture guilt-free chicken skeweres seasoned to perfection, or classic black pudding with apple slices for a real kick. And let's not forget those air-fried Haggis Bites with a delightful balsamic glaze, a tasty, low-carb side dish that's sure to impress. Give these a go and transform your starters and sides into something sensational!

Chicken Sausage and Bell Pepper Skewers

NUTRITION INFORMATION

- *Calories: 350 kcal*
- *Carbohydrates: 14g*
- *Protein: 28g*
- *Fats: 20g*
- *Sugar: 6g*
- *Sodium: 450mg*

DIRECTIONS:

1. Preheat the air fryer to 200°C (392°F).
2. Thread the chicken sausages and bell pepper chunks onto skewers, alternating between sausage and peppers.
3. Drizzle the skewers with olive oil* (optional) and season with salt and pepper.
4. Place the skewers in the air fryer basket in a single layer.
5. Air fry for 12-15 minutes, turning halfway through, until the chicken sausages are cooked through and the bell peppers are tender and slightly charred.
6. Remove the skewers from the air fryer and let them cool slightly before serving.
7. Enjoy your delicious Chicken Sausage and Bell Pepper Skewers!

This recipe contains a healthy highlight that we don't recommend you switch with other ingredients

INGREDIENTS

- *2 chicken sausages**
- *1 red bell pepper, cut into chunks*
- *1 yellow bell pepper, cut into chunks*
- *1 green bell pepper, cut into chunks*
- *1 tablespoon olive oil* (optional)*
- *Salt and pepper to taste*

Using the measurements above will make exactly one serving of this meal. This serving size will match the nutritional information on this page.

Healthy Highlights:

WHOLE GRAIN | HEALTHY FATS | LEAN PROTEIN

Mini Cheese and Onion Pie

NUTRITION INFORMATION

- Calories: 250 kcal
- Carbohydrates: 20g
- Protein: 10g
- Fats: 15g
- Sugar: 2g
- Sodium: 300mg

DIRECTIONS:

1. Preheat the air fryer to 180°C (356°F).
2. Roll out the puff pastry and cut into small circles.
3. In a pan, sauté the chopped onion in olive oil* until translucent.
4. Place a spoonful of sautéed onions and grated cheese* in the center of each pastry circle.
5. Fold the pastry over to form mini pies and seal the edges with a fork.
6. Place the mini pies in the air fryer basket in a single layer.
7. Air fry for 10-12 minutes or until the pastry is golden brown and crispy.
8. Remove the mini pies from the air fryer and let them cool slightly before serving.
9. Enjoy your tasty Mini Cheese and Onion Pies!

* This recipe contains a healthy highlight that we don't recommend you switch with other ingredients

INGREDIENTS

- 1 sheet whole grain puff pastry*
- 50g grated cheese
- 1 small onion, finely chopped
- 1 tablespoon olive oil* (optional)
- Salt and pepper to taste

Using the measurements above will make exactly one serving of this meal. This serving size will match the nutritional information on this page.

Healthy Highlights:

- WHOLE GRAIN
- HEALTHY FATS
- LEAN PROTEIN

Whole Grain Crispy Cheese and Spinach Rolls

NUTRITION INFORMATION

- Calories: 200 kcal
- Carbohydrates: 15g
- Protein: 8g
- Fats: 12g
- Sugar: 2g
- Sodium: 250mg

DIRECTIONS:

1. Preheat the air fryer to 180°C (356°F).
2. Lay out the tortillas and sprinkle grated cheese evenly over each tortilla.
3. Place fresh spinach leaves on top of the cheese.
4. Roll up the tortillas tightly and secure with toothpicks.
5. Brush the rolls with olive oil* (optional) and season with salt and pepper.
6. Place the rolls in the air fryer basket in a single layer.
7. Air fry for 8-10 minutes or until the rolls are golden and crispy.
8. Remove the rolls from the air fryer and let them cool slightly before serving.
9. Enjoy your wholesome Whole Grain Crispy Cheese and Spinach Rolls!

INGREDIENTS

- 4 whole grain tortillas*
- 100g grated cheese
- 100g fresh spinach leaves
- 1 tablespoon olive oil* (optional)
- Salt and pepper to taste

Using the measurements above will make exactly one serving of this meal. This serving size will match the nutritional information on this page.

*This recipe contains a healthy highlight that we don't recommend you switch with other ingredients

Healthy Highlights:

- WHOLE GRAIN
- HEALTHY FATS
- LEAN PROTEIN

Mini Cornish Pasties with Cauliflower Crust

NUTRITION INFORMATION

- Calories: 180 kcal
- Carbohydrates: 15g
- Protein: 8g
- Fats: 10g
- Sugar: 3g
- Sodium: 280mg

DIRECTIONS:

1. Preheat the air fryer to 180°C (356°F).
2. In a bowl, mix cauliflower rice*, lean minced beef*, diced potato, chopped onion, olive oil* (optional), salt, and pepper.
3. Divide the mixture into small portions and shape into mini pasties.
4. Place the mini pasties in the air fryer basket in a single layer.
5. Air fry for 15-20 minutes or until the pasties are cooked through and golden brown.
6. Remove the pasties from the air fryer and let them cool slightly before serving.
7. Enjoy your delightful Mini Cornish Pasties with Cauliflower Crust!

This recipe contains a healthy highlight that we don't recommend you switch with other ingredients

INGREDIENTS

- 1 cup cauliflower rice*
- 100g lean minced beef*
- 1 small potato, diced
- 1 small onion, finely chopped
- 1 tablespoon olive oil* (optional)
- Salt and pepper to taste

Using the measurements above will make exactly one serving of this meal. This serving size will match the nutritional information on this page.

Healthy Highlights:

- WHOLE GRAIN
- HEALTHY FATS
- LEAN PROTEIN

Black Pudding and Apple Slices

NUTRITION INFORMATION

- *Calories: 180 kcal*
- *Carbohydrates: 15g*
- *Protein: 8g*
- *Fats: 10g*
- *Sugar: 5g*
- *Sodium: 300mg*

DIRECTIONS:

1. Preheat the air fryer to 200°C (392°F).
2. Brush both sides of the black pudding slices and apple slices with olive oil* (optional).
3. Season with salt and pepper.
4. Place the black pudding slices and apple slices in the air fryer basket in a single layer.
5. Air fry for 8-10 minutes or until the black pudding is crispy and the apple slices are tender.
6. Remove from the air fryer and let them cool slightly before serving.
7. Enjoy your scrumptious Black Pudding and Apple Slices!

This recipe contains a healthy highlight that we don't recommend you switch with other ingredients

INGREDIENTS

- *2 slices black pudding**
- *1 apple, thinly sliced*
- *1 tablespoon olive oil* (optional)*
- *Salt and pepper to taste*

Using the measurements above will make exactly one serving of this meal. This serving size will match the nutritional information on this page.

Healthy Highlights:

WHOLE GRAIN | HEALTHY FATS | LEAN PROTEIN

Welsh Rarebit Stuffed Portobello

NUTRITION INFORMATION

- *Calories: 220 kcal*
- *Carbohydrates: 10g*
- *Protein: 12g*
- *Fats: 15g*
- *Sugar: 2g*
- *Sodium: 350mg*

DIRECTIONS:

1. Preheat the air fryer to 180°C (356°F).
2. Remove the stems from the Portobello mushrooms and place them in the air fryer basket.
3. In a bowl, mix grated cheddar cheese, toasted bread cubes, Worcestershire sauce, olive oil* (optional), salt, and pepper.
4. Stuff the mushroom caps with the cheese mixture.
5. Place the stuffed mushrooms in the air fryer basket.
6. Air fry for 12-15 minutes or until the mushrooms are cooked and the cheese is melted and golden.
7. Remove from the air fryer and let them cool slightly before serving.
8. Enjoy your delightful Welsh Rarebit Stuffed Portobello!

* This recipe contains a healthy highlight that we don't recommend you switch with other ingredients

INGREDIENTS

- *2 large Portobello mushrooms*
- *50g grated cheddar cheese*
- *2 slices whole grain bread*, toasted and cubed*
- *1 tablespoon Worcestershire sauce*
- *1 tablespoon olive oil* (optional)*
- *Salt and pepper to taste*

Using the measurements above will make exactly one serving of this meal. This serving size will match the nutritional information on this page.

Healthy Highlights:

WHOLE GRAIN | HEALTHY FATS | LEAN PROTEIN

Fish Goujons

NUTRITION INFORMATION

- Calories: 250 kcal
- Carbohydrates: 20g
- Protein: 15g
- Fats: 12g
- Sugar: 2g
- Sodium: 350mg

DIRECTIONS:

1. Preheat the air fryer to 200°C (392°F).
2. Dip the fish strips into the beaten egg, then coat with breadcrumbs*.
3. Drizzle olive oil* (optional) over the fish strips and season with salt and pepper.
4. Place the fish strips in the air fryer basket in a single layer.
5. Air fry for 10-12 minutes or until the fish is golden and crispy.
6. Remove from the air fryer and let them cool slightly before serving.
7. Enjoy your delicious Fish Goujons!

*This recipe contains a healthy highlight that we don't recommend you switch with other ingredients

INGREDIENTS

- 2 fillets of white fish (such as cod or haddock), cut into strips*
- 1 egg, beaten
- 50g breadcrumbs (whole grain if available)*
- 1 tablespoon olive oil* (optional)
- Salt and pepper to taste

Using the measurements above will make exactly one serving of this meal. This serving size will match the nutritional information on this page.

Healthy Highlights:

- WHOLE GRAIN
- HEALTHY FATS
- LEAN PROTEIN

27

Crispy Haggis Bites

NUTRITION INFORMATION

- Calories: 180 kcal
- Carbohydrates: 10g
- Protein: 8g
- Fats: 10g
- Sugar: 2g
- Sodium: 300mg

DIRECTIONS:

1. Preheat the air fryer to 180°C (356°F).
2. Toss the haggis cubes with olive oil* (optional), salt, and pepper.
3. Place the haggis cubes in the air fryer basket in a single layer.
4. Air fry for 10-12 minutes or until the haggis is crispy and golden.
5. Remove from the air fryer and let them cool slightly before serving.
6. Enjoy your crispy Haggis Bites!

INGREDIENTS

- 200g haggis, cut into small cubes*
- 1 tablespoon olive oil* (optional)
- Salt and pepper to taste

Using the measurements above will make exactly one serving of this meal. This serving size will match the nutritional information on this page.

Healthy Highlights:

- WHOLE GRAIN
- HEALTHY FATS
- LEAN PROTEIN

* This recipe contains a healthy highlight that we don't recommend you switch with other ingredients

Mini Yorkshire Puddings with Roasted Zucchini

NUTRITION INFORMATION

- *Calories: 180 kcal*
- *Carbohydrates: 15g*
- *Protein: 8g*
- *Fats: 10g*
- *Sugar: 2g*
- *Sodium: 250mg*

DIRECTIONS:

1. Preheat the air fryer to 200°C (392°F).
2. In a bowl, whisk together the plain flour, egg, and milk to make the batter.
3. Drizzle olive oil* (optional) over the sliced zucchini and season with salt and pepper.
4. Place the zucchini slices in the air fryer basket in a single layer.
5. Spoon the batter into mini muffin moulds in the air fryer basket, filling them halfway.
6. Air fry the zucchini slices for 8-10 minutes until tender and golden.
7. Add the mini muffin moulds to the air fryer and continue to air fry for another 10-12 minutes or until the Yorkshire puddings are risen and golden.
8. Remove from the air fryer and let them cool slightly before serving.
9. Enjoy your delightful Mini Yorkshire Puddings with Roasted Zucchini!

This recipe contains a healthy highlight that we don't recommend you switch with other ingredients

INGREDIENTS

- 100g plain flour
- 1 egg
- 100ml milk
- 1 small zucchini, sliced
- 1 tablespoon olive oil* (optional)
- Salt and pepper to taste

Using the measurements above will make exactly one serving of this meal. This serving size will match the nutritional information on this page.

Healthy Highlights:

WHOLE GRAIN | HEALTHY FATS | LEAN PROTEIN

Turkey Scotch Eggs

NUTRITION INFORMATION

- *Calories: 220 kcal*
- *Carbohydrates: 10g*
- *Protein: 18g*
- *Fats: 12g*
- *Sugar: 2g*
- *Sodium: 350mg*

DIRECTIONS:

1. *Preheat the air fryer to 180°C (356°F).*
2. *Peel the hard-boiled eggs and set aside.*
3. *Mix the turkey mince* with breadcrumbs*, olive oil* (optional), salt, and pepper.*
4. *Divide the mixture into two portions.*
5. *Flatten each portion and wrap around one hard-boiled egg to form a scotch egg.*
6. *Place the scotch eggs in the air fryer basket in a single layer.*
7. *Air fry for 15-18 minutes*
8. *Remove from the air fryer and let them cool slightly before serving.*
9. *Enjoy your delectable Turkey Scotch Eggs*

* This recipe contains a healthy highlight that we don't recommend you switch with other ingredients

INGREDIENTS

- *2 hard-boiled eggs*
- *200g turkey mince**
- *50g breadcrumbs (whole grain if available)**
- *1 tablespoon olive oil* (optional)*
- *Salt and pepper to taste*

Using the measurements above will make exactly one serving of this meal. This serving size will match the nutritional information on this page.

Healthy Highlights:

- WHOLE GRAIN
- HEALTHY FATS
- LEAN PROTEIN

Poultry Recipes

Savour healthy and flavourful poultry dishes made effortlessly in the air fryer.

Imagine juicy air-fried chicken thighs marinated in zesty lemon and herbs, or fragrant goose breast cooked with rosemary and garlic for a low-carb delight. How about a delicious turkey meatloaf, both heart-healthy and diabetes-friendly? These recipes are set to become your new favourites, so get cooking and enjoy every bite!

Chicken and Vegetable Pie

NUTRITION INFORMATION

- Calories: 400 kcal
- Carbohydrates: 35g
- Protein: 25g
- Fats: 18g
- Sugar: 5g
- Sodium: 400mg

DIRECTIONS:

1. Preheat the air fryer to 180°C (356°F).
2. In a pan, heat olive oil* (optional) and sauté onion* until translucent.
3. Add diced potato*, carrot*, and peas* to the pan. Cook until vegetables are tender.
4. Add diced chicken breast* to the pan and season with salt and pepper.
5. Roll out puff pastry* and cut into a circle slightly larger than your pie dish.
6. Place the cooked chicken and vegetable mixture into the pie dish.
7. Cover with puff pastry*, crimping the edges to seal.
8. Brush the pastry with beaten egg* (egg wash).
9. Place the pie in the air fryer basket.
10. Air fry for 20-25 minutes or until the pastry is golden and crisp.
11. Remove from the air fryer and let it cool slightly before serving.
12. Enjoy your Chicken and Vegetable Pie!

* This recipe contains a healthy highlight that we don't recommend you switch with other ingredients

INGREDIENTS

- 200g cooked chicken breast*, diced
- 1 medium potato*, peeled and diced
- 1 carrot*, diced
- 1 onion*, chopped
- 100g peas*
- 1 tablespoon olive oil* (optional)
- Salt and pepper to taste
- 1 sheet ready-made puff pastry*
- 1 egg, beaten* (for egg wash)

Using the measurements above will make exactly one serving of this meal. This serving size will match the nutritional information on this page.

Healthy Highlights:

WHOLE GRAIN | HEALTHY FATS | LEAN PROTEIN

Lemon Herb Chicken Thighs

NUTRITION INFORMATION

- *Calories: 300 kcal*
- *Carbohydrates: 5g*
- *Protein: 30g*
- *Fats: 18g*
- *Sugar: 2g*
- *Sodium: 350mg*

DIRECTIONS:

1. Preheat the air fryer to 180°C (356°F).
2. In a bowl, mix lemon juice, lemon zest, minced garlic, olive oil*, chopped fresh herbs, salt, and pepper.
3. Rub the lemon herb mixture over the chicken thighs*, ensuring they are well coated.
4. Place the chicken thighs* in the air fryer basket, skin side up.
5. Air fry for 25-30 minutes or until the chicken is cooked through and the skin is crispy.
6. Remove from the air fryer and let it rest for a few minutes before serving.
7. Enjoy your flavourful Lemon Herb Chicken Thighs!

* This recipe contains a healthy highlight that we don't recommend you switch with other ingredients

INGREDIENTS

- *2 chicken thighs*, skin on*
- *1 lemon, juiced and zested*
- *2 cloves garlic, minced*
- *1 tablespoon olive oil**
- *Fresh herbs (such as rosemary, thyme)*
- *Salt and pepper to taste*

Using the measurements above will make exactly one serving of this meal. This serving size will match the nutritional information on this page.

Healthy Highlights:

WHOLE GRAIN | HEALTHY FATS | LEAN PROTEIN

Chicken and Spinach Stuffed Peppers

NUTRITION INFORMATION

- Calories: 250 kcal
- Carbohydrates: 15g
- Protein: 20g
- Fats: 12g
- Sugar: 5g
- Sodium: 300mg

DIRECTIONS:

1. Preheat the air fryer to 180°C (356°F).
2. In a pan, heat olive oil* and sauté onion and garlic until softened.
3. Add spinach leaves to the pan and cook until wilted.
4. Stir in shredded chicken breast* and season with salt and pepper.
5. Fill each bell pepper half with the chicken and spinach mixture.
6. If using, sprinkle grated cheese on top of each stuffed pepper.
7. Place the stuffed peppers in the air fryer basket.
8. Air fry for 15-20 minutes or until the peppers are tender and the cheese is melted and bubbly.
9. Remove from the air fryer and let them cool slightly before serving.
10. Enjoy your delicious Chicken and Spinach Stuffed Peppers!

*This recipe contains a healthy highlight that we don't recommend you switch with other ingredients

INGREDIENTS

- 2 bell peppers, halved and deseeded
- 200g cooked chicken breast*, shredded
- 100g spinach leaves
- 1 onion, chopped
- 2 cloves garlic, minced
- 1 tablespoon olive oil*
- Salt and pepper to taste
- 50g grated cheese (optional)

Using the measurements above will make exactly one serving of this meal. This serving size will match the nutritional information on this page.

Healthy Highlights:

- WHOLE GRAIN
- HEALTHY FATS
- LEAN PROTEIN

Tikka Skewers and Cauliflower Rice

NUTRITION INFORMATION

- Calories: 350 kcal
- Carbohydrates: 15g
- Protein: 25g
- Fats: 20g
- Sugar: 6g
- Sodium: 450mg

DIRECTIONS:

1. Preheat the air fryer to 200°C (392°F).
2. In a bowl, combine cubed chicken breasts*, bell pepper chunks, red onion chunks, tikka spice mix, olive oil* (optional), salt, and pepper. Mix well to coat the chicken and vegetables.
3. Thread the marinated chicken and vegetables onto skewers, alternating between chicken, peppers, and onions.
4. Place the skewers in the air fryer basket in a single layer.
5. Air fry for 12-15 minutes or until the chicken is cooked through and the vegetables are tender and slightly charred.
6. While the skewers are cooking, grate the cauliflower to make cauliflower rice.
7. Heat a pan over medium heat and add the grated cauliflower Stir-fry for 5-7 minutes until tender.
8. Serve the tikka skewers on a bed of cauliflower rice.
9. Garnish with fresh coriander leaves (optional) before serving.
10. Enjoy your flavourful Tikka Skewers with Cauliflower Rice!

* This recipe contains a healthy highlight that we don't recommend you switch with other ingredients

INGREDIENTS

- 2 chicken breasts*, cubed
- 1 bell pepper, cut into chunks
- 1 red onion, cut into chunks
- 100g cauliflower*, grated
- 1 tablespoon olive oil* (optional)
- Tikka spice mix
- Salt and pepper to taste
- Fresh coriander leaves (optional, for garnish)

Using the measurements above will make exactly one serving of this meal. This serving size will match the nutritional information on this page.

Healthy Highlights:

WHOLE GRAIN | HEALTHY FATS | LEAN PROTEIN

Broccoli Stuffed Chicken Breasts

NUTRITION INFORMATION

- Calories: 300 kcal
- Carbohydrates: 10g
- Protein: 30g
- Fats: 15g
- Sugar: 4g
- Sodium: 400mg

DIRECTIONS:

1. Preheat the air fryer to 180°C (356°F).
2. Use a sharp knife to butterfly each chicken breast*, creating a pocket for stuffing.
3. In a bowl, mix steamed and chopped broccoli florets*, minced garlic*, grated cheese* (optional), olive oil* (optional), salt, and pepper.
4. Stuff each chicken breast* with the broccoli mixture, then secure with toothpicks.
5. Place the stuffed chicken breasts in the air fryer basket.
6. Air fry for 20-25 minutes or until the chicken is cooked through and golden.
7. Remove from the air fryer and let them rest for a few minutes before serving.
8. Enjoy your tasty Broccoli Stuffed Chicken Breasts!

This recipe contains a healthy highlight that we don't recommend you switch with other ingredients

INGREDIENTS

- 2 chicken breasts*, boneless and skinless
- 100g broccoli florets, steamed and chopped
- 50g grated cheese (optional)
- 2 cloves garlic, minced
- 1 tablespoon olive oil* (optional)
- Salt and pepper to taste

Using the measurements above will make exactly one serving of this meal. This serving size will match the nutritional information on this page.

Healthy Highlights:

- WHOLE GRAIN
- HEALTHY FATS
- LEAN PROTEIN

Honey Mustard Chicken Drumsticks

NUTRITION INFORMATION

- Calories: 280 kcal
- Carbohydrates: 10g
- Protein: 25g
- Fats: 15g
- Sugar: 8g
- Sodium: 350mg

DIRECTIONS:

1. Preheat the air fryer to 180°C (356°F).
2. In a bowl, mix honey*, whole grain mustard*, olive oil*, salt, and pepper.
3. Brush the honey mustard mixture over the chicken drumsticks* to coat evenly.
4. Place the drumsticks in the air fryer basket.
5. Air fry for 25-30 minutes or until the chicken is cooked through and golden.
6. Remove from the air fryer and let them rest for a few minutes before serving.
7. Enjoy your delicious Honey Mustard Chicken Drumsticks!

* This recipe contains a healthy highlight that we don't recommend you switch with other ingredients

INGREDIENTS

- 2 chicken drumsticks*
- 2 tablespoons honey
- 1 tablespoon whole grain mustard
- 1 tablespoon olive oil*
- Salt and pepper to taste

Using the measurements above will make exactly one serving of this meal. This serving size will match the nutritional information on this page.

Healthy Highlights:

- WHOLE GRAIN
- HEALTHY FATS
- LEAN PROTEIN

Goose Breast with Rosemary and Garlic

NUTRITION INFORMATION

- *Calories: 320 kcal*
- *Carbohydrates: 5g*
- *Protein: 30g*
- *Fats: 20g*
- *Sugar: 0g*
- *Sodium: 400mg*

DIRECTIONS:

1. *Preheat the air fryer to 180°C (356°F).*
2. *Season the goose breast fillet* with minced garlic*, fresh rosemary leaves*, olive oil*, salt, and pepper.*
3. *Place the seasoned goose breast in the air fryer basket.*
4. *Air fry for 15-20 minutes or until the goose breast is cooked through and the skin is crispy.*
5. *Remove from the air fryer and let it rest for a few minutes before serving.*
6. *Slice the goose breast and serve with your favourite side dishes.*
7. *Enjoy your flavourful Goose Breast with Rosemary and Garlic!*

* This recipe contains a healthy highlight that we don't recommend you switch with other ingredients

INGREDIENTS

- *1 goose breast fillet**
- *2 cloves garlic, minced*
- *Fresh rosemary leaves*
- *1 tablespoon olive oil**
- *Salt and pepper to taste*

Using the measurements above will make exactly one serving of this meal. This serving size will match the nutritional information on this page.

Healthy Highlights:

- WHOLE GRAIN
- HEALTHY FATS
- LEAN PROTEIN

Goose Meatballs

NUTRITION INFORMATION

- Calories: 250 kcal
- Carbohydrates: 10g
- Protein: 20g
- Fats: 15g
- Sugar: 2g
- Sodium: 350mg

DIRECTIONS:

1. Preheat the air fryer to 180°C (356°F).
2. In a bowl, mix goose mince*, chopped onion*, minced garlic*, egg*, breadcrumbs*, chopped parsley*, olive oil*, salt, and pepper.
3. Roll the mixture into meatballs of equal size.
4. Place the meatballs in the air fryer basket.
5. Air fry for 15-18 minutes or until the meatballs are cooked through and golden brown.
6. Remove from the air fryer and let them rest for a few minutes before serving.
7. Serve the goose meatballs with your preferred sauce or accompaniments.
8. Enjoy your tasty Goose Meatballs!

INGREDIENTS

- 200g goose mince*
- 1 onion, finely chopped
- 2 cloves garlic, minced
- 1 egg
- 50g breadcrumbs (whole grain if available)*
- Fresh parsley, chopped
- 1 tablespoon olive oil
- Salt and pepper to taste

Using the measurements above will make exactly one serving of this meal. This serving size will match the nutritional information on this page.

Healthy Highlights:

- WHOLE GRAIN
- HEALTHY FATS
- LEAN PROTEIN

*This recipe contains a healthy highlight that we don't recommend you switch with other ingredients

Turkey & Cranberry Stuffed Mushrooms

NUTRITION INFORMATION

- Calories: 180 kcal
- Carbohydrates: 10g
- Protein: 15g
- Fats: 8g
- Sugar: 3g
- Sodium: 300mg

DIRECTIONS:

1. Preheat the air fryer to 180°C (356°F).
2. In a bowl, mix shredded turkey breast*, cranberry sauce*, grated cheese* (optional), chopped parsley*, salt, and pepper.
3. Fill each mushroom cap with the turkey and cranberry mixture.
4. Place the stuffed mushrooms in the air fryer basket.
5. Air fry for 12-15 minutes or until the mushrooms are tender and the filling is heated through.
6. Remove from the air fryer and let them cool slightly before serving.
7. Enjoy your delightful Turkey and Cranberry Stuffed Mushrooms!

* This recipe contains a healthy highlight that we don't recommend you switch with other ingredients

INGREDIENTS

- 4 large mushrooms, stems removed
- 100g cooked turkey breast*, shredded
- 2 tablespoons cranberry sauce
- 50g grated cheese (optional)
- Fresh parsley, chopped
- Salt and pepper to taste

Using the measurements above will make exactly one serving of this meal. This serving size will match the nutritional information on this page.

Healthy Highlights:

- WHOLE GRAIN
- HEALTHY FATS
- LEAN PROTEIN

Turkey and Apricot Meatloaf Minis

NUTRITION INFORMATION

- *Calories: 220 kcal*
- *Carbohydrates: 15g*
- *Protein: 18g*
- *Fats: 10g*
- *Sugar: 4g*
- *Sodium: 350mg*

DIRECTIONS:

1. Preheat the air fryer to 180°C (356°F).
2. In a bowl, combine lean turkey mince*, breadcrumbs*, egg*, chopped dried apricots*, olive oil*, salt, and pepper. Mix until well combined.
3. Shape the mixture into mini meatloaves.
4. Place the meatloaf minis in the air fryer basket.
5. Air fry for 20-25 minutes or until the meatloaves are cooked through and golden brown.
6. Remove from the air fryer and let them rest for a few minutes before serving.
7. Enjoy your delicious Turkey and Apricot Meatloaf Minis!

* This recipe contains a healthy highlight that we don't recommend you switch with other ingredients

INGREDIENTS

- *200g lean turkey mince**
- *50g breadcrumbs (whole grain if available)**
- *1 egg*
- *2 tablespoons dried apricots, finely chopped*
- *1 tablespoon olive oil**
- *Salt and pepper to taste*

Using the measurements above will make exactly one serving of this meal. This serving size will match the nutritional information on this page.

Healthy Highlights:

WHOLE GRAIN | HEALTHY FATS | LEAN PROTEIN

Beef Recipes

Dive into hearty and satisfying beef recipes perfect for diabetics, all made in the air fryer.

Envision crunchy beef and sweet potato pattie with a side of mashed cauliflower, or a juicy air-fried beef kofta with cumin and coriander. For something different, try beef and cauliflower tots packed with nutrition and flavour. These dishes are a must-try, so fire up your air fryer and get ready to enjoy!

Beef and Sweet Potato Pattie

NUTRITION INFORMATION

- *Calories: 350 kcal*
- *Carbohydrates: 25g*
- *Protein: 20g*
- *Fats: 18g*
- *Sugar: 5g*
- *Sodium: 400mg*

DIRECTIONS:

1. Preheat the air fryer to 180°C (356°F).
2. In a bowl, combine lean beef mince*, grated sweet potato*, chopped onion*, minced garlic*, wholemeal flour*, egg*, salt, and pepper.
3. Mix until well combined, then form the mixture into patties.
4. Brush the patties with olive oil* (optional).
5. Place the patties in the air fryer basket.
6. Air fry for 15-18 minutes or until cooked through and golden brown.
7. Remove from the air fryer and let them rest for a few minutes before serving.
8. Enjoy your Beef and Sweet Potato Pattie!

* This recipe contains a healthy highlight that we don't recommend you switch with other ingredients

INGREDIENTS

- 150g lean beef mince*
- 1 small sweet potato, grated
- 1 onion, finely chopped
- 1 clove garlic, minced
- 1 tablespoon wholemeal flour*
- 1 egg
- Salt and pepper to taste
- 1 tablespoon olive oil* (optional)

Using the measurements above will make exactly one serving of this meal. This serving size will match the nutritional information on this page.

Healthy Highlights:

- WHOLE GRAIN
- HEALTHY FATS
- LEAN PROTEIN

Beef Fajita Strips

NUTRITION INFORMATION

- Calories: 300 kcal
- Carbohydrates: 15g
- Protein: 25g
- Fats: 15g
- Sugar: 5g
- Sodium: 450mg

DIRECTIONS:

1. Preheat the air fryer to 200°C (392°F).
2. In a bowl, toss lean beef strips*, sliced bell pepper*, sliced onion*, olive oil*, chili powder, ground cumin, salt, and pepper until well coated.
3. Place the beef and vegetable mixture in the air fryer basket.
4. Air fry for 10-12 minutes or until the beef is cooked through and the vegetables are tender and slightly charred.
5. Warm the wholemeal tortilla wrap* (optional) in the air fryer for a few minutes.
6. Serve the beef fajita strips with warm tortilla wraps* and enjoy!

This recipe contains a healthy highlight that we don't recommend you switch with other ingredients

INGREDIENTS

- 200g lean beef strips*
- 1 bell pepper, sliced
- 1 onion, sliced
- 1 tablespoon olive oil*
- 1 teaspoon chili powder
- 1 teaspoon ground cumin
- Salt and pepper to taste
- Wholemeal tortilla wrap* (optional)

Using the measurements above will make exactly one serving of this meal. This serving size will match the nutritional information on this page.

Healthy Highlights:

- WHOLE GRAIN
- HEALTHY FATS
- LEAN PROTEIN

Meatballs with Zucchini Noodles

NUTRITION INFORMATION

- Calories: 320 kcal
- Carbohydrates: 20g
- Protein: 25g
- Fats: 15g
- Sugar: 6g
- Sodium: 400mg

DIRECTIONS:

1. Preheat the air fryer to 180°C (356°F).
2. In a bowl, mix lean beef mince*, egg*, breadcrumbs*, minced garlic*, dried oregano, salt, and pepper.
3. Shape the mixture into meatballs.
4. Brush the meatballs with olive oil*.
5. Place the meatballs in the air fryer basket.
6. Air fry for 15-18 minutes or until the meatballs are cooked through and golden brown.
7. Meanwhile, spiralize the zucchini* to make zucchini noodles.
8. Place in air fryer to heat the spiralized zucchini*.
9. Cook for 3-4 minutes until tender.
10. Serve the meatballs with zucchini noodles and enjoy!

This recipe contains a healthy highlight that we don't recommend you switch with other ingredients

INGREDIENTS

- 200g lean beef mince*
- 1 egg
- 2 tablespoons breadcrumbs (whole grain if available)*
- 1 clove garlic, minced
- 1 teaspoon dried oregano
- Salt and pepper to taste
- 1 tablespoon olive oil*
- 1 zucchini, spiralized

Using the measurements above will make exactly one serving of this meal. This serving size will match the nutritional information on this page.

Healthy Highlights:

WHOLE GRAIN | HEALTHY FATS | LEAN PROTEIN

Beef Koftas

NUTRITION INFORMATION

- Calories: 280 kcal
- Carbohydrates: 10g
- Protein: 20g
- Fats: 18g
- Sugar: 4g
- Sodium: 350mg

DIRECTIONS:

1. Preheat the air fryer to 180°C (356°F).
2. In a bowl, mix lean beef mince*, grated onion*, minced garlic*, ground cumin, ground coriander, paprika, salt, and pepper.
3. Shape the mixture into kofta shapes.
4. Brush the koftas with olive oil* (optional).
5. Place the koftas in the air fryer basket.
6. Air fry for 15-18 minutes or until cooked through and browned.
7. Remove from the air fryer and let them rest for a few minutes before serving.
8. Enjoy your tasty Beef Koftas!

*This recipe contains a healthy highlight that we don't recommend you switch with other ingredients

INGREDIENTS

- 200g lean beef mince*
- 1 onion, grated
- 2 cloves garlic, minced
- 1 teaspoon ground cumin
- 1 teaspoon ground coriander
- 1 teaspoon paprika
- Salt and pepper to taste
- 1 tablespoon olive oil* (optional)

Using the measurements above will make exactly one serving of this meal. This serving size will match the nutritional information on this page.

Healthy Highlights:

WHOLE GRAIN | HEALTHY FATS | LEAN PROTEIN

Beef and Cauliflower Tater Tot

NUTRITION INFORMATION

- Calories: 250 kcal
- Carbohydrates: 15g
- Protein: 20g
- Fats: 12g
- Sugar: 3g
- Sodium: 300mg

DIRECTIONS:

1. Preheat the air fryer to 180°C (356°F).
2. In a bowl, mix lean beef mince*, grated cauliflower*, egg*, wholemeal flour*, grated cheese* (optional), salt, and pepper.
3. Form the mixture into small tater tot shapes.
4. Brush the tater tots with olive oil* (optional).
5. Place the tater tots in the air fryer basket.
6. Air fry for 12-15 minutes or until golden and crispy.
7. Remove from the air fryer and let them cool slightly before serving.
8. Enjoy your Beef and Cauliflower Tater Tots!

* This recipe contains a healthy highlight that we don't recommend you switch with other ingredients

INGREDIENTS

- 150g lean beef mince*
- 100g cauliflower, grated
- 1 egg
- 1 tablespoon wholemeal flour*
- 1 tablespoon grated cheese (optional)
- Salt and pepper to taste
- 1 tablespoon olive oil* (optional)

Using the measurements above will make exactly one serving of this meal. This serving size will match the nutritional information on this page.

Healthy Highlights:

- WHOLE GRAIN
- HEALTHY FATS
- LEAN PROTEIN

Welsh Beef and Swede Pasties

NUTRITION INFORMATION

- Calories: 320 kcal
- Carbohydrates: 20g
- Protein: 25g
- Fats: 15g
- Sugar: 4g
- Sodium: 380mg

DIRECTIONS:

1. Preheat the air fryer to 180°C (356°F).
2. In a pan, heat olive oil* and sauté onion*, carrot*, potato*, and swede* until tender.
3. Add lean beef mince* to the pan and cook until browned.
4. Season with salt and pepper, then let the mixture cool slightly.
5. Roll out the puff pastry* and cut into squares.
6. Spoon the beef and vegetable mixture onto one half of each puff pastry square.
7. Fold the other half of the pastry over the filling to create a pasty shape.
8. Press the edges to seal, then brush with beaten egg* (egg wash).
9. Place the pasties in the air fryer basket.
10. Air fry for 20-25 minutes or until golden and crispy.
11. Remove from the air fryer and let them cool before serving.
12. Enjoy your Welsh Beef and Swede Pasties!

This recipe contains a healthy highlight that we don't recommend you switch with other ingredients

INGREDIENTS

- 200g lean beef mince*
- 1 swede, diced
- 1 onion, chopped
- 1 carrot, diced
- 1 potato*, diced
- 1 tablespoon olive oil*
- Salt and pepper to taste
- 1 sheet ready-made puff pastry* (wholemeal if available)
- 1 egg, beaten

Using the measurements above will make exactly one serving of this meal. This serving size will match the nutritional information on this page.

Healthy Highlights:

WHOLE GRAIN | HEALTHY FATS | LEAN PROTEIN

Beef and Leek Cakes

NUTRITION INFORMATION

- *Calories: 280 kcal*
- *Carbohydrates: 18g*
- *Protein: 20g*
- *Fats: 15g*
- *Sugar: 3g*
- *Sodium: 350mg*

DIRECTIONS:

1. Preheat the air fryer to 180°C (356°F).
2. In a bowl, mix lean beef mince*, chopped leek*, chopped onion*, wholemeal flour*, egg*, salt, and pepper.
3. Shape the mixture into small cakes.
4. Brush the cakes with olive oil* (optional).
5. Place the cakes in the air fryer basket.
6. Air fry for 15-18 minutes or until cooked through and golden brown.
7. Remove from the air fryer and let them rest for a few minutes before serving.
8. Enjoy your Beef and Leek Cakes!

* This recipe contains a healthy highlight that we don't recommend you switch with other ingredients

INGREDIENTS

- *200g lean beef mince**
- *1 leek, finely chopped*
- *1 onion, chopped*
- *1 tablespoon wholemeal flour**
- *1 egg*
- *Salt and pepper to taste*
- *1 tablespoon olive oil* (optional)*

Using the measurements above will make exactly one serving of this meal. This serving size will match the nutritional information on this page.

Healthy Highlights:

WHOLE GRAIN | HEALTHY FATS | LEAN PROTEIN

Beef and Pearl Barley Rissole

NUTRITION INFORMATION

- *Calories: 300 kcal*
- *Carbohydrates: 25g*
- *Protein: 20g*
- *Fats: 15g*
- *Sugar: 3g*
- *Sodium: 380mg*

DIRECTIONS:

1. Preheat the air fryer to 180°C (356°F).
2. Cook pearl barley* according to package instructions until tender.
3. In a pan, heat olive oil* and sauté chopped onion* and minced garlic* until softened.
4. In a bowl, combine cooked pearl barley*, sautéed onion* and garlic*, lean beef mince*, wholemeal flour*, egg*, salt, and pepper.
5. Shape the mixture into rissole shapes.
6. Brush the rissoles with olive oil* (optional).
7. Place the rissoles in the air fryer basket.
8. Air fry for 15-18 minutes or until cooked through and golden brown.
9. Remove from the air fryer and let them rest for a few minutes before serving.
10. Enjoy your Beef and Pearl Barley Rissole!

* This recipe contains a healthy highlight that we don't recommend you switch with other ingredients

INGREDIENTS

- *200g lean beef mince**
- *50g pearl barley**
- *1 onion, chopped*
- *1 clove garlic, minced*
- *1 tablespoon wholemeal flour**
- *1 egg*
- *Salt and pepper to taste*
- *1 tablespoon olive oil* (optional)*

Using the measurements above will make exactly one serving of this meal. This serving size will match the nutritional information on this page.

Healthy Highlights:

WHOLE GRAIN | HEALTHY FATS | LEAN PROTEIN

Beef and Cabbage Rolls

NUTRITION INFORMATION

- Calories: 280 kcal
- Carbohydrates: 20g
- Protein: 22g
- Fats: 12g
- Sugar: 5g
- Sodium: 350mg

DIRECTIONS:

1. Preheat the air fryer to 180°C (356°F).
2. Blanch cabbage leaves* in boiling water for a few minutes until soft. Drain and set aside.
3. In a pan, heat olive oil* and sauté chopped onion* and minced garlic* until softened.
4. In a bowl, mix lean beef mince*, sautéed onion* and garlic*, wholemeal breadcrumbs*, egg*, salt, and pepper.
5. Divide the beef mixture into four portions.
6. Place a portion of the beef mixture onto each cabbage leaf and roll up, tucking in the sides.
7. Brush the cabbage rolls with olive oil* (optional).
8. Place the cabbage rolls in the air fryer basket.
9. Air fry for 15-18 minutes or until cooked through and browned.
10. Remove from the air fryer and let them rest for a few minutes before serving.
11. Enjoy your Beef and Cabbage Rolls!

* This recipe contains a healthy highlight that we don't recommend you switch with other ingredients

INGREDIENTS

- 200g lean beef mince*
- 4 large cabbage leaves
- 1 onion, chopped
- 1 clove garlic, minced
- 1 tablespoon wholemeal breadcrumbs*
- 1 egg
- Salt and pepper to taste
- 1 tablespoon olive oil* (optional)

Using the measurements above will make exactly one serving of this meal. This serving size will match the nutritional information on this page.

Healthy Highlights:

- WHOLE GRAIN
- HEALTHY FATS
- LEAN PROTEIN

Welsh Rarebit Beef Burgers

NUTRITION INFORMATION

- *Calories: 320 kcal*
- *Carbohydrates: 20g*
- *Protein: 24g*
- *Fats: 15g*
- *Sugar: 4g*
- *Sodium: 400mg*

DIRECTIONS:

1. Preheat the air fryer to 180°C (356°F).
2. In a bowl, combine lean beef mince*, toasted and crumbled wholemeal bread*, grated cheese* (optional), Worcestershire sauce, mustard, egg*, salt, and pepper.
3. Shape the mixture into a burger patty.
4. Brush the burger patty with olive oil* (optional).
5. Place the burger patty in the air fryer basket.
6. Air fry for 15-18 minutes or until cooked through and golden.
7. Remove from the air fryer and let it rest for a few minutes before serving.
8. Enjoy your delicious Welsh Rarebit Beef Burger!

* This recipe contains a healthy highlight that we don't recommend you switch with other ingredients

INGREDIENTS

- *150g lean beef mince**
- *1 slice wholemeal bread*, toasted and crumbled*
- *1 tablespoon grated cheese (optional)*
- *1 tablespoon Worcestershire sauce*
- *1 teaspoon mustard*
- *1 egg*
- *Salt and pepper to taste*
- *1 tablespoon olive oil* (optional)*

Using the measurements above will make exactly one serving of this meal. This serving size will match the nutritional information on this page.

Healthy Highlights:

WHOLE GRAIN | HEALTHY FATS | LEAN PROTEIN

Pork Recipes

Relish in delicious pork dishes that won't spike your blood sugar, thanks to the air fryer.

Picture succulent pork barbecue with guilt-free sauce, or a savoury air-fried pork cutlet covered with almond flour. And for a treat, try ribeye with a fiesty mustard glazet for a low-carb diet. These recipes are too good to miss, so let's get cooking and savour every mouthful!

Stuffed Pork Loin with Spinach & Feta

NUTRITION INFORMATION

- *Calories: 320 kcal*
- *Carbohydrates: 10g*
- *Protein: 30g*
- *Fats: 18g*
- *Sugar: 2g*
- *Sodium: 350mg*

DIRECTIONS:

1. Preheat the air fryer to 180°C (356°F).
2. Butterfly the pork loin* by cutting it horizontally without cutting all the way through.
3. Season the inside with salt, pepper, and minced garlic*.
4. Place fresh spinach* and crumbled feta cheese* inside the pork loin*.
5. Close the pork loin* and tie with kitchen twine to secure the filling.
6. Brush the pork loin* with olive oil* (optional).
7. Place the stuffed pork loin* in the air fryer basket.
8. Air fry for 25-30 minutes or until the pork is cooked through and golden brown.
9. Remove from the air fryer and let it rest for a few minutes before slicing.
10. Enjoy your Stuffed Pork Loin with Spinach and Feta!

* This recipe contains a healthy highlight that we don't recommend you switch with other ingredients

INGREDIENTS

- *200g pork loin*
- *50g fresh spinach*
- *30g feta cheese*
- *1 clove garlic, minced*
- *Salt and pepper to taste*
- *1 tablespoon olive oil* (optional)*

Using the measurements above will make exactly one serving of this meal. This serving size will match the nutritional information on this page.

Healthy Highlights:

- WHOLE GRAIN
- HEALTHY FATS
- LEAN PROTEIN

Pork Ribs with Sugar-Free BBQ Sauce

NUTRITION INFORMATION

- Calories: 380 kcal
- Carbohydrates: 5g
- Protein: 25g
- Fats: 28g
- Sugar: 1g
- Sodium: 450mg

DIRECTIONS:

1. Preheat the air fryer to 200°C (392°F).
2. Season the pork ribs* with salt and pepper.
3. Place the pork ribs* in the air fryer basket.
4. Air fry for 25-30 minutes, turning halfway through, until the ribs are cooked and tender.
5. Brush the pork ribs* with sugar-free BBQ sauce*.
6. Air fry for an additional 5 minutes to caramelize the sauce.
7. Remove from the air fryer and let them rest for a few minutes before serving.
8. Enjoy your Pork Ribs with Sugar-Free BBQ Sauce!

* This recipe contains a healthy highlight that we don't recommend you switch with other ingredients

INGREDIENTS

- 250g pork ribs
- Sugar-free BBQ sauce
- Salt and pepper to taste

Using the measurements above will make exactly one serving of this meal. This serving size will match the nutritional information on this page.

Healthy Highlights:

- WHOLE GRAIN
- HEALTHY FATS
- LEAN PROTEIN

Spiced Pork Collar Steaks with Avocado Salsa

NUTRITION INFORMATION

- *Calories: 340 kcal*
- *Carbohydrates: 10g*
- *Protein: 25g*
- *Fats: 22g*
- *Sugar: 3g*
- *Sodium: 400mg*

DIRECTIONS:

1. Preheat the air fryer to 200°C (392°F).
2. Season the pork collar steaks* with spices (paprika, cumin, garlic powder, chili powder), salt, and pepper.
3. Place the pork collar steaks* in the air fryer basket.
4. Air fry for 12-15 minutes or until cooked through and golden.
5. In a bowl, mix diced avocado*, diced tomato*, finely chopped red onion*, chopped fresh coriander*, lime juice, salt, and pepper to make the avocado salsa.
6. Heat olive oil* (optional) in a pan and sauté the avocado salsa for a few minutes.
7. Serve the spiced pork collar steaks* with avocado salsa on top.
8. Enjoy your Spiced Pork Collar Steaks with Avocado Salsa!

This recipe contains a healthy highlight that we don't recommend you switch with other ingredients

INGREDIENTS

- 2 pork collar steaks
- 1 avocado*, diced
- 1 tomato, diced
- 1/4 red onion finely chopped
- Fresh coriander, chopped
- 1 lime, juiced
- Salt and pepper to taste
- 1 tablespoon olive oil* (optional)
- Spices (paprika, cumin, garlic powder, chili powder)

Using the measurements above will make exactly one serving of this meal. This serving size will match the nutritional information on this page.

Healthy Highlights:

WHOLE GRAIN | HEALTHY FATS | LEAN PROTEIN

Pork Cutlets with Almond Flour Breading

NUTRITION INFORMATION

- Calories: 300 kcal
- Carbohydrates: 10g
- Protein: 30g
- Fats: 15g
- Sugar: 1g
- Sodium: 350mg

DIRECTIONS:

1. Preheat the air fryer to 180°C (356°F).
2. Season the pork cutlets* with salt and pepper.
3. Beat the egg* in a bowl.
4. Dip each pork cutlet* into the beaten egg*, then coat with almond flour*.
5. Brush the coated pork cutlets* with olive oil* (optional).
6. Place the pork cutlets* in the air fryer basket.
7. Air fry for 12-15 minutes or until golden and cooked through.
8. Remove from the air fryer and let them rest for a few minutes before serving.
9. Enjoy your Pork Cutlets with Almond Flour Breading!

* This recipe contains a healthy highlight that we don't recommend you switch with other ingredients

INGREDIENTS

- 2 pork cutlets
- 50g almond flour*
- 1 egg
- Salt and pepper to taste
- 1 tablespoon olive oil* (optional)

Using the measurements above will make exactly one serving of this meal. This serving size will match the nutritional information on this page.

Healthy Highlights:

WHOLE GRAIN — HEALTHY FATS — LEAN PROTEIN

Honey-Ginger Pork Tenderloin Skewers

NUTRITION INFORMATION

- *Calories: 320 kcal*
- *Carbohydrates: 15g*
- *Protein: 25g*
- *Fats: 15g*
- *Sugar: 12g*
- *Sodium: 300mg*

DIRECTIONS:

1. Preheat the air fryer to 200°C (392°F).
2. In a bowl, mix honey*, grated ginger*, soy sauce, salt, and pepper.
3. Thread the pork tenderloin* cubes onto the soaked wooden skewers.
4. Brush the skewers with the honey-ginger mixture.
5. Place the skewers in the air fryer basket.
6. Air fry for 10-12 minutes, turning halfway through, until the pork is cooked and caramelized.
7. Remove from the air fryer and let them rest for a few minutes before serving.
8. Enjoy your Honey-Ginger Pork Tenderloin Skewers!

INGREDIENTS

- *200g pork tenderloin, cut into cubes*
- *2 tablespoons honey*
- *1 tablespoon grated ginger*
- *1 tablespoon soy sauce (low sodium)*
- *Salt and pepper to taste*
- *Wooden skewers, soaked in water*

Using the measurements above will make exactly one serving of this meal. This serving size will match the nutritional information on this page.

Healthy Highlights:

WHOLE GRAIN | HEALTHY FATS | LEAN PROTEIN

* This recipe contains a healthy highlight that we don't recommend you switch with other ingredients

Garlic-Herb Pork Sirloin Roast

NUTRITION INFORMATION

- Calories: 280 kcal
- Carbohydrates: 10g
- Protein: 30g
- Fats: 12g
- Sugar: 1g
- Sodium: 300mg

DIRECTIONS:

1. Preheat the air fryer to 180°C (356°F).
2. Rub minced garlic*, chopped fresh herbs*, salt, and pepper onto the pork sirloin roast*.
3. Drizzle olive oil* (optional) over the seasoned roast.
4. Place the pork sirloin roast* in the air fryer basket.
5. Air fry for 25-30 minutes or until the pork is cooked to your desired doneness.
6. Remove from the air fryer and let it rest for a few minutes before slicing.
7. Enjoy your Garlic-Herb Pork Sirloin Roast!

*This recipe contains a healthy highlight that we don't recommend you switch with other ingredients

INGREDIENTS

- 250g pork sirloin roast
- 2 cloves garlic, minced
- Fresh herbs (rosemary, thyme, sage), chopped
- Salt and pepper to taste
- 1 tablespoon olive oil* (optional)

Using the measurements above will make exactly one serving of this meal. This serving size will match the nutritional information on this page.

Healthy Highlights:

WHOLE GRAIN | HEALTHY FATS | LEAN PROTEIN

Spicy Pork Sausage Patties with Cauliflower Mash

NUTRITION INFORMATION

- Calories: 340 kcal
- Carbohydrates: 15g
- Protein: 25g
- Fats: 20g
- Sugar: 3g
- Sodium: 400mg

DIRECTIONS:

1. Preheat the air fryer to 180°C (356°F).
2. In a bowl, mix pork sausage meat*, chili flakes, paprika, cumin, salt, and pepper.
3. Shape the mixture into patties.
4. Place the patties in the air fryer basket.
5. Air fry for 12-15 minutes, turning halfway through, until the patties are cooked through and browned.
6. Meanwhile, steam cauliflower* until tender and mash with butter*.
7. Serve the spicy pork sausage patties on a bed of cauliflower mash.
8. Garnish with chopped fresh parsley* (optional) and drizzle with olive oil* (optional).
9. Enjoy your Spicy Pork Sausage Patties with Cauliflower Mash!

*This recipe contains a healthy highlight that we don't recommend you switch with other ingredients

INGREDIENTS

- 200g pork sausage meat
- 1/2 teaspoon chili flakes
- 1/2 teaspoon paprika
- 1/4 teaspoon cumin
- Salt and pepper to taste
- 200g cauliflower, steamed and mashed
- 1 tablespoon butter
- Fresh parsley, chopped (optional)
- 1 tablespoon olive oil* (optional)

Using the measurements above will make exactly one serving of this meal. This serving size will match the nutritional information on this page.

Healthy Highlights:

WHOLE GRAIN | HEALTHY FATS | LEAN PROTEIN

Pork Ribeye Steaks with Mustard Glaze

NUTRITION INFORMATION

- *Calories: 360 kcal*
- *Carbohydrates: 5g*
- *Protein: 30g*
- *Fats: 25g*
- *Sugar: 2g*
- *Sodium: 380mg*

DIRECTIONS:

1. Preheat the air fryer to 200°C (392°F).
2. Season the pork ribeye steaks* with salt and pepper.
3. Mix Dijon mustard (sugar-free)* with honey* (optional) to make the glaze.
4. Brush the glaze onto both sides of the pork ribeye steaks*.
5. Place the steaks in the air fryer basket.
6. Air fry for 10-12 minutes or until the steaks are cooked to your desired doneness.
7. Remove from the air fryer and let them rest for a few minutes before serving.
8. Enjoy your Pork Ribeye Steaks with Mustard Glaze!

*This recipe contains a healthy highlight that we don't recommend you switch with other ingredients

INGREDIENTS

- 2 pork ribeye steaks
- 2 tablespoons Dijon mustard (sugar-free)
- 1 tablespoon honey (optional)
- Salt and pepper to taste
- 1 tablespoon olive oil* (optional)

Using the measurements above will make exactly one serving of this meal. This serving size will match the nutritional information on this page.

Healthy Highlights:

WHOLE GRAIN | HEALTHY FATS | LEAN PROTEIN

Belly Strips with Smoky Paprika Rub

NUTRITION INFORMATION

- *Calories: 320 kcal*
- *Carbohydrates: 5g*
- *Protein: 28g*
- *Fats: 22g*
- *Sugar: 1g*
- *Sodium: 350mg*

DIRECTIONS:

1. Preheat the air fryer to 180°C (356°F).
2. Season the pork belly strips* with smoky paprika, salt, and pepper.
3. Drizzle olive oil* (optional) over the seasoned strips.
4. Place the strips in the air fryer basket.
5. Air fry for 15-18 minutes or until the strips are crispy and cooked through.
6. Remove from the air fryer and let them rest for a few minutes before serving.
7. Enjoy your Belly Strips with Smoky Paprika Rub!

INGREDIENTS

- *200g pork belly strips*
- *Smoky paprika*
- *Salt and pepper to taste*
- *1 tablespoon olive oil* (optional)*

Using the measurements above will make exactly one serving of this meal. This serving size will match the nutritional information on this page.

Healthy Highlights:

WHOLE GRAIN · HEALTHY FATS · LEAN PROTEIN

* This recipe contains a healthy highlight that we don't recommend you switch with other ingredients

Pork Loin Chops with Herb Crust

NUTRITION INFORMATION

- Calories: 340 kcal
- Carbohydrates: 10g
- Protein: 30g
- Fats: 18g
- Sugar: 1g
- Sodium: 380mg

DIRECTIONS:

1. Preheat the air fryer to 180°C (356°F).
2. In a bowl, mix wholemeal breadcrumbs*, chopped fresh herbs*, minced garlic*, salt, and pepper.
3. Press the herb mixture onto both sides of the pork loin chops* to form a crust.
4. Drizzle olive oil* (optional) over the chops.
5. Place the chops in the air fryer basket.
6. Air fry for 12-15 minutes or until the chops are cooked through and the crust is golden.
7. Remove from the air fryer and let them rest for a few minutes before serving.
8. Enjoy your Pork Loin Chops with Herb Crust!

INGREDIENTS

- 2 pork loin chops
- 50g wholemeal breadcrumbs*
- Fresh herbs (parsley, thyme, rosemary), chopped
- 1 clove garlic, minced
- Salt and pepper to taste
- 1 tablespoon olive oil* (optional)

Using the measurements above will make exactly one serving of this meal. This serving size will match the nutritional information on this page.

Healthy Highlights:

WHOLE GRAIN | HEALTHY FATS | LEAN PROTEIN

* This recipe contains a healthy highlight that we don't recommend you switch with other ingredients

Lamb Recipes

Indulge in rich and flavourful lamb recipes that are diabetes-friendly and easy to make in the air fryer.

Think of air-fried lamb cutlets marinated in mint pesto, or a tender lamb shoulder with balsamic glaze. For a hearty balanced meal, prepare lamb meat with a refreshing yogurt sauce in a delicious sandwich. These dishes are sure to delight, so give them a try and enjoy the sumptuous flavours!

Herb-Crusted Lamb Chops

NUTRITION INFORMATION

- *Calories: 350 kcal*
- *Carbohydrates: 10g*
- *Protein: 25g*
- *Fats: 22g*
- *Sugar: 2g*
- *Sodium: 300mg*

DIRECTIONS:

1. Preheat the air fryer to 200°C (392°F).
2. In a bowl, mix wholemeal breadcrumbs*, chopped fresh herbs*, minced garlic*, salt, and pepper.
3. Press the herb mixture onto both sides of the lamb chops* to form a crust.
4. Drizzle olive oil* (optional) over the chops.
5. Place the chops in the air fryer basket.
6. Air fry for 12-15 minutes or until the chops are cooked to your desired doneness and the crust is golden.
7. Remove from the air fryer and let them rest for a few minutes before serving.
8. Enjoy your Herb-Crusted Lamb Chops!

INGREDIENTS

- *2 lamb chops**
- *50g wholemeal breadcrumbs**
- *Fresh herbs (rosemary, thyme), chopped*
- *1 clove garlic, minced*
- *Salt and pepper to taste*
- *1 tablespoon olive oil* (optional)*

* This recipe contains a healthy highlight that we don't recommend you switch with other ingredients

Healthy Highlights:

WHOLE GRAIN | HEALTHY FATS | LEAN PROTEIN

Rosemary Lamb Shoulder

NUTRITION INFORMATION

- *Calories: 320 kcal*
- *Carbohydrates: 5g*
- *Protein: 30g*
- *Fats: 20g*
- *Sugar: 1g*
- *Sodium: 350mg*

DIRECTIONS:

1. Preheat the air fryer to 180°C (356°F).
2. Make small incisions in the lamb shoulder* and insert fresh rosemary* sprigs and minced garlic*.
3. Season the lamb shoulder* with salt and pepper.
4. Drizzle olive oil* (optional) over the shoulder.
5. Place the lamb shoulder* in the air fryer basket.
6. Air fry for 25-30 minutes or until the lamb is cooked through and tender.
7. Remove from the air fryer and let it rest for a few minutes before slicing.
8. Enjoy your Rosemary Lamb Shoulder!

*This recipe contains a healthy highlight that we don't recommend you switch with other ingredients

INGREDIENTS

- *200g lamb shoulder**
- *Fresh rosemary sprigs*
- *1 clove garlic, minced*
- *Salt and pepper to taste*
- *1 tablespoon olive oil* (optional)*

Using the measurements above will make exactly one serving of this meal. This serving size will match the nutritional information on this page.

Healthy Highlights:

WHOLE GRAIN | HEALTHY FATS | LEAN PROTEIN

Lamb Koftas with Tzatziki Sauce

NUTRITION INFORMATION

- Calories: 300 kcal
- Carbohydrates: 10g
- Protein: 25g
- Fats: 18g
- Sugar: 3g
- Sodium: 350mg

DIRECTIONS:

1. Preheat the air fryer to 200°C (392°F).
2. In a bowl, mix lamb mince*, grated onion*, minced garlic*, ground cumin, ground coriander, salt, and pepper.
3. Divide the mixture into 4 portions and shape each into a kofta.
4. Brush the koftas with olive oil* (optional).
5. Place the koftas in the air fryer basket.
6. Air fry for 12-15 minutes or until cooked through and browned.
7. Serve the lamb koftas with tzatziki sauce*.
8. Enjoy your Lamb Koftas with Tzatziki Sauce!

INGREDIENTS

- 250g lamb mince*
- 1/4 onion, grated
- 1 clove garlic, minced
- 1 teaspoon ground cumin
- 1 teaspoon ground coriander
- Salt and pepper to taste
- 1 tablespoon olive oil* (optional)
- Tzatziki sauce (to serve)

Using the measurements above will make exactly one serving of this meal. This serving size will match the nutritional information on this page.

Healthy Highlights:

WHOLE GRAIN | HEALTHY FATS | LEAN PROTEIN

* This recipe contains a healthy highlight that we don't recommend you switch with other ingredients

Tomato Zucchini Pasta with Lamb Meatballs

NUTRITION INFORMATION

- *Calories: 300*
- *Carbohydrates: 25g*
- *Protein: 10g*
- *Fats: 18g*
- *Sugar: 8g*
- *Sodium: 100mg*

DIRECTIONS:

1. Preheat the air fryer to 180°C (356°F).
2. In a bowl, mix lamb mince*, wholemeal breadcrumbs*, egg*, minced garlic*, salt, and pepper.
3. Shape the mixture into meatballs.
4. Brush the meatballs with olive oil* (optional).
5. Place the meatballs in the air fryer basket.
6. Air fry for 15-18 minutes or until cooked through and browned.
7. Meanwhile, spiralize the zucchini* and halve the cherry tomatoes*.
8. In a pan, sauté the spiralized zucchini* and cherry tomatoes* until tender.
9. Serve the tomato zucchini pasta with lamb meatballs on top.
10. Garnish with chopped fresh basil* (optional).
11. Enjoy your Tomato Zucchini Pasta with Lamb Meatballs!

* This recipe contains a healthy highlight that we don't recommend you switch with other ingredients

INGREDIENTS

- 200g lamb mince*
- 1/4 cup wholemeal breadcrumbs*
- 1 egg
- 1 clove garlic, minced
- Salt and pepper to taste
- 1 tablespoon olive oil* (optional)
- 1 zucchini, spiralized
- 1/2 cup cherry tomatoes, halved
- Fresh basil, chopped (optional)

Using the measurements above will make exactly one serving of this meal. This serving size will match the nutritional information on this page.

Healthy Highlights:

- WHOLE GRAIN
- HEALTHY FATS
- LEAN PROTEIN

Lamb Cutlets with Mint Pesto

NUTRITION INFORMATION

- Calories: 340 kcal
- Carbohydrates: 5g
- Protein: 28g
- Fats: 22g
- Sugar: 1g
- Sodium: 380mg

DIRECTIONS:

1. Preheat the air fryer to 200°C (392°F).
2. Season the lamb cutlets* with salt and pepper.
3. In a food processor, combine fresh mint leaves*, minced garlic*, pine nuts*, grated Parmesan cheese*, salt, and pepper to make the mint pesto.
4. Brush the lamb cutlets* with olive oil* (optional).
5. Place the cutlets in the air fryer basket.
6. Air fry for 12-15 minutes or until cooked to your desired doneness.
7. Remove from the air fryer and let them rest for a few minutes before serving.
8. Serve the lamb cutlets with mint pesto on top.
9. Enjoy your Lamb Cutlets with Mint Pesto!

*This recipe contains a healthy highlight that we don't recommend you switch with other ingredients

INGREDIENTS

- 2 lamb cutlets*
- Fresh mint leaves
- 1 clove garlic, minced
- 1 tablespoon pine nuts*
- 1 tablespoon grated Parmesan cheese
- Salt and pepper to taste
- 1 tablespoon olive oil* (optional)

Using the measurements above will make exactly one serving of this meal. This serving size will match the nutritional information on this page.

Healthy Highlights:

- WHOLE GRAIN
- HEALTHY FATS
- LEAN PROTEIN

Lamb Shoulder Chops with Balsamic Glaze

NUTRITION INFORMATION

- Calories: 360 kcal
- Carbohydrates: 10g
- Protein: 30g
- Fats: 25g
- Sugar: 2g
- Sodium: 380mg

DIRECTIONS:

1. Preheat the air fryer to 200°C (392°F).
2. Season the lamb shoulder chops* with salt and pepper.
3. Drizzle balsamic glaze* over the chops.
4. Brush the chops with olive oil* (optional).
5. Place the chops in the air fryer basket.
6. Air fry for 12-15 minutes or until cooked through and caramelized.
7. Remove from the air fryer and let them rest for a few minutes before serving.
8. Enjoy your Lamb Shoulder Chops with Balsamic Glaze!

INGREDIENTS

- 2 lamb shoulder chops*
- Balsamic glaze
- Salt and pepper to taste
- 1 tablespoon olive oil* (optional)

Using the measurements above will make exactly one serving of this meal. This serving size will match the nutritional information on this page.

Healthy Highlights:

WHOLE GRAIN | HEALTHY FATS | LEAN PROTEIN

* This recipe contains a healthy highlight that we don't recommend you switch with other ingredients

Garlic Lamb Shank with Mashed Cauliflower

NUTRITION INFORMATION

- Calories: 340 kcal
- Carbohydrates: 15g
- Protein: 25g
- Fats: 18g
- Sugar: 3g
- Sodium: 300mg

DIRECTIONS:

1. Preheat the air fryer to 180°C (356°F).
2. Rub minced garlic*, fresh rosemary* sprigs, salt, and pepper onto the lamb shank*.
3. Place the lamb shank* in the air fryer basket.
4. Air fry for 30-35 minutes or until the lamb is tender and cooked through.
5. Meanwhile, steam cauliflower* until tender and mash with butter* (optional).
6. Serve the garlic lamb shank with mashed cauliflower.
7. Enjoy your Garlic Lamb Shank with Mashed Cauliflower!

INGREDIENTS

- 1 lamb shank*
- 1 clove garlic, minced
- Fresh rosemary sprigs
- Salt and pepper to taste
- 200g cauliflower, steamed and mashed
- 1 tablespoon butter (optional)

Using the measurements above will make exactly one serving of this meal. This serving size will match the nutritional information on this page.

Healthy Highlights:

- WHOLE GRAIN
- HEALTHY FATS
- LEAN PROTEIN

* This recipe contains a healthy highlight that we don't recommend you switch with other ingredients

Lamb Eggplant Rolls

NUTRITION INFORMATION

- *Calories: 320 kcal*
- *Carbohydrates: 10g*
- *Protein: 25g*
- *Fats: 20g*
- *Sugar: 3g*
- *Sodium: 350mg*

DIRECTIONS:

1. *Preheat the air fryer to 200°C (392°F).*
2. *In a bowl, mix lamb mince*, tomato sauce (sugar-free), grated Parmesan cheese, chopped parsley* (optional), salt, and pepper.*
3. *Lay out the eggplant* slices and spoon the lamb mixture onto each slice.*
4. *Roll up the eggplant* slices to form rolls.*
5. *Brush the rolls with olive oil* (optional).*
6. *Place the rolls in the air fryer basket.*
7. *Air fry for 15-18 minutes or until the rolls are cooked through and golden.*
8. *Remove from the air fryer and let them rest for a few minutes before serving.*
9. *Enjoy your Lamb Eggplant Rolls!*

INGREDIENTS

- *200g lamb mince**
- *1 eggplant, thinly sliced lengthwise*
- *1/4 cup tomato sauce (sugar-free)*
- *1/4 cup grated Parmesan cheese*
- *Fresh parsley, chopped (optional)*
- *Salt and pepper to taste*
- *1 tablespoon olive oil* (optional)*

Using the measurements above will make exactly one serving of this meal. This serving size will match the nutritional information on this page.

Healthy Highlights:

WHOLE GRAIN | HEALTHY FATS | LEAN PROTEIN

* This recipe contains a healthy highlight that we don't recommend you switch with other ingredients

Traditional Welsh Lamb Cawl

NUTRITION INFORMATION

- *Calories: 350 kcal*
- *Carbohydrates: 20g*
- *Protein: 25g*
- *Fats: 18g*
- *Sugar: 5g*
- *Sodium: 400mg*

DIRECTIONS:

1. Preheat the air fryer to 180°C (356°F).
2. In the air fryer, put olive oil* (optional, onion*, carrots*, and leek* until softened.
3. Add diced lamb leg* and brown for a few minutes.
4. Add potatoes*, pearl barley*, salt, pepper.
5. Cook for 30 minutes or until the lamb and vegetables are tender.
6. Serve the Welsh lamb cawl garnished with chopped fresh parsley* (optional).
7. Enjoy your Traditional Welsh Lamb Cawl!

INGREDIENTS

- *200g lamb leg*, diced*
- *1 onion, chopped*
- *2 carrots, sliced*
- *1 leek, sliced*
- *2 potatoes, diced*
- *1/2 cup pearl barley**
- *1 tablespoon olive oil* (optional)*
- *Fresh parsley, chopped (optional)*
- *Salt and pepper to taste*

Using the measurements above will make exactly one serving of this meal. This serving size will match the nutritional information on this page.

* This recipe contains a healthy highlight that we don't recommend you switch with other ingredients

Healthy Highlights:

- WHOLE GRAIN
- HEALTHY FATS
- LEAN PROTEIN

Lamb Yogurt Sauce Sandwich

NUTRITION INFORMATION

- *Calories: 320 kcal*
- *Carbohydrates: 25g*
- *Protein: 20g*
- *Fats: 15g*
- *Sugar: 8g*
- *Sodium: 350mg*

DIRECTIONS:

1. Preheat the air fryer to 180°C (356°F). Cook lamb slices for 15-18 minutes.
2. Spread Greek yogurt* on one slice of whole grain bread*.
3. Layer lettuce leaves*, tomato slices*, cucumber slices*, and cooked lamb* on top.
4. Sprinkle chopped fresh mint leaves* over the lamb.
5. Season with salt and pepper.
6. Cover with the other slice of whole grain bread*.
7. Slice the sandwich in half.
8. Serve your Lamb Yogurt Sauce Sandwich!

INGREDIENTS

- *100g cooked lamb*, sliced*
- *2 slices whole grain bread**
- *Lettuce leaves*
- *Tomato slices*
- *Cucumber slices*
- *2 tablespoons Greek yogurt**
- *Fresh mint leaves, chopped*
- *Salt and pepper to taste*

Using the measurements above will make exactly one serving of this meal. This serving size will match the nutritional information on this page.

Healthy Highlights:

- WHOLE GRAIN
- HEALTHY FATS
- LEAN PROTEIN

* This recipe contains a healthy highlight that we don't recommend you switch with other ingredients

Fish Recipes

Treat yourself to healthy and delicious fish recipes cooked perfectly in the air fryer.

Imagine crispy air-fried plaice with almond crust, or flaky haddock fish sticks with spiced cauliflower. You can also prepare quick and easy air-fried cod with a spicy curry marinade. These recipes are a catch, so get frying and enjoy the taste of the sea!

Cod with Lemon and Herbs

NUTRITION INFORMATION

- *Calories: 250*
- *Carbohydrates: 5g*
- *Protein: 30g*
- *Fats: 12g*
- *Sugar: 1g*
- *Sodium: 300mg*

DIRECTIONS:

1. Preheat the air fryer to 180°C (356°F) for 3 minutes.
2. Pat dry the cod fillet and season it with salt and pepper.
3. Drizzle the olive oil and lemon juice over the cod.
4. Sprinkle fresh herbs on top.
5. Place the cod in the air fryer basket.
6. Cook for 10-12 minutes until the fish is cooked through and flakes easily with a fork.
7. Serve hot with a side of steamed vegetables or a small salad.

INGREDIENTS

- 150g cod fillet*
- 1 tablespoon lemon juice
- 1 teaspoon olive oil*
- Fresh herbs (such as parsley, thyme, and rosemary)
- Salt and pepper to taste

Using the measurements above will make exactly one serving of this meal. This serving size will match the nutritional information on this page.

Healthy Highlights:

WHOLE GRAIN | HEALTHY FATS | LEAN PROTEIN

* This recipe contains a healthy highlight that we don't recommend you switch with other ingredients

Haddock Fish and Chips

NUTRITION INFORMATION

- Calories: 350
- Carbohydrates: 30g
- Protein: 25g
- Fats: 15g
- Sugar: 1g
- Sodium: 400mg

DIRECTIONS:

1. Preheat the air fryer to 200°C (392°F) for 3 minutes.
2. Toss the potato chips with olive oil, salt, and pepper.
3. Place the haddock fillet and potato chips in the air fryer basket.
4. Cook for 15-18 minutes until the fish is cooked and the chips are golden and crispy, shaking the basket halfway through cooking.
5. Serve hot with a side of steamed peas or a small salad.

*This recipe contains a healthy highlight that we don't recommend you switch with other ingredients

INGREDIENTS

- 150g haddock fillet*
- 1 medium potato, cut into chips
- 1 teaspoon olive oil*
- Salt and pepper to taste

Using the measurements above will make exactly one serving of this meal. This serving size will match the nutritional information on this page.

Healthy Highlights:

- WHOLE GRAIN
- HEALTHY FATS
- LEAN PROTEIN

Haddock with Spiced Cauliflower

NUTRITION INFORMATION

- *Calories: 300*
- *Carbohydrates: 20g*
- *Protein: 28g*
- *Fats: 14g*
- *Sugar: 5g*
- *Sodium: 350mg*

DIRECTIONS:

1. Preheat the air fryer to 200°C (392°F) for 3 minutes.
2. Toss the cauliflower florets with olive oil, paprika, cumin, salt, and pepper.
3. Place the haddock fillet and spiced cauliflower in the air fryer basket.
4. Cook for 12-15 minutes until the fish is cooked through and the cauliflower is tender, shaking the basket halfway through cooking.
5. Serve hot with a squeeze of lemon juice.

INGREDIENTS

- *150g haddock fillet**
- *150g cauliflower florets*
- *1 teaspoon olive oil**
- *1 teaspoon paprika*
- *1/2 teaspoon cumin*
- *Salt and pepper to taste*

Using the measurements above will make exactly one serving of this meal. This serving size will match the nutritional information on this page.

Healthy Highlights:

WHOLE GRAIN | HEALTHY FATS | LEAN PROTEIN

* This recipe contains a healthy highlight that we don't recommend you switch with other ingredients

Salmon with Asparagus

NUTRITION INFORMATION

- Calories: 280
- Carbohydrates: 8g
- Protein: 30g
- Fats: 15g
- Sugar: 4g
- Sodium: 350mg

DIRECTIONS:

1. Preheat the air fryer to 180°C (356°F) for 3 minutes.
2. Drizzle olive oil over the salmon fillet and season with lemon zest, salt, and pepper.
3. Place the salmon fillet and asparagus spears in the air fryer basket.
4. Cook for 10-12 minutes until the salmon is cooked to your desired doneness and the asparagus is tender.
5. Serve hot with a side of quinoa or brown rice.

*This recipe contains a healthy highlight that we don't recommend you switch with other ingredients

INGREDIENTS

- 150g salmon fillet*
- 100g asparagus spears
- 1 teaspoon olive oil*
- Lemon zest
- Salt and pepper to taste

Using the measurements above will make exactly one serving of this meal. This serving size will match the nutritional information on this page.

Healthy Highlights:

WHOLE GRAIN | HEALTHY FATS | LEAN PROTEIN

Mackerel with Lemon Dill Sauce

NUTRITION INFORMATION

- Calories: 280
- Carbohydrates: 2g
- Protein: 25g
- Fats: 18g
- Sugar: 1g
- Sodium: 300mg

DIRECTIONS:

1. Preheat the air fryer to 180°C (356°F) for 3 minutes.
2. Season the mackerel fillet with salt and pepper.
3. Place the mackerel in the air fryer basket and cook for 8-10 minutes until cooked through and crispy.
4. In a small bowl, mix Greek yogurt, lemon juice, chopped dill, salt, and pepper to make the sauce.
5. Serve the mackerel hot with the lemon dill sauce drizzled on top.

INGREDIENTS

- 150g mackerel fillet*
- 1 tablespoon Greek yogurt*
- 1 teaspoon lemon juice
- 1/2 teaspoon fresh dill, chopped
- Salt and pepper to taste

Using the measurements above will make exactly one serving of this meal. This serving size will match the nutritional information on this page.

Healthy Highlights:

WHOLE GRAIN | HEALTHY FATS | LEAN PROTEIN

* This recipe contains a healthy highlight that we don't recommend you switch with other ingredients

Plaice with Almond Crust

NUTRITION INFORMATION

- ◆ *Calories: 320*
- ◆ *Carbohydrates: 10g*
- ◆ *Protein: 30g*
- ◆ *Fats: 18g*
- ◆ *Sugar: 2g*
- ◆ *Sodium: 350mg*

DIRECTIONS:

1. Preheat the air fryer to 180°C (356°F) for 3 minutes.
2. Mix almond meal, olive oil, garlic powder, salt, and pepper to make a crust.
3. Pat the plaice fillet dry and coat it with the almond crust mixture.
4. Place the plaice in the air fryer basket and cook for 10-12 minutes until the fish is cooked through and the crust is golden and crispy.
5. Serve hot with a side of steamed vegetables or a small salad.

INGREDIENTS

- ◆ *150g plaice fillet**
- ◆ *2 tablespoons almond meal**
- ◆ *1 teaspoon olive oil**
- ◆ *1/2 teaspoon garlic powder*
- ◆ *Salt and pepper to taste*

Using the measurements above will make exactly one serving of this meal. This serving size will match the nutritional information on this page.

Healthy Highlights:

WHOLE GRAIN | HEALTHY FATS | LEAN PROTEIN

* This recipe contains a healthy highlight that we don't recommend you switch with other ingredients

Mixed Fish Pie

NUTRITION INFORMATION

- Calories: 350
- Carbohydrates: 25g
- Protein: 30g
- Fats: 15g
- Sugar: 4g
- Sodium: 400mg

DIRECTIONS:

1. Preheat the air fryer to 180°C (356°F) for 3 minutes.
2. Cook the mixed fish in the air fryer for 10 minutes until cooked through.
3. In a separate bowl, mix mashed potato, skimmed milk, butter, salt, pepper, and fresh herbs (if using) to make the topping.
4. Place the cooked fish in a baking dish and top with the mashed potato mixture.
5. Air fry for another 5-7 minutes until the topping is golden and crispy.
6. Serve hot with a side of steamed vegetables.

INGREDIENTS

- 150g mixed fish (such as cod, haddock, and salmon)*
- 1 small potato, mashed
- 1/4 cup skimmed milk
- 1 teaspoon butter
- Salt and pepper to taste
- Fresh herbs (optional)

Using the measurements above will make exactly one serving of this meal. This serving size will match the nutritional information on this page.

Healthy Highlights:

WHOLE GRAIN HEALTHY FATS LEAN PROTEIN

* This recipe contains a healthy highlight that we don't recommend you switch with other ingredients

Cod and Cauliflower Fishcakes

NUTRITION INFORMATION
- Calories: 280
- Carbohydrates: 15g
- Protein: 25g
- Fats: 12g
- Sugar: 3g
- Sodium: 350mg

DIRECTIONS:
1. Preheat the air fryer to 180°C (356°F) for 3 minutes.
2. Cook the cod fillet in the air fryer for 8-10 minutes until cooked through.
3. In a bowl, combine the cooked cauliflower, breadcrumbs, beaten egg, fresh herbs, salt, and pepper to form a mixture.
4. Divide the mixture into small patties and coat with a little olive oil.
5. Place the fishcakes in the air fryer basket and cook for 10-12 minutes until golden and crispy.
6. Serve hot with a side of salad or steamed vegetables.

*This recipe contains a healthy highlight that we don't recommend you switch with other ingredients

INGREDIENTS
- 150g cod fillet*
- 100g cauliflower, steamed and mashed
- 1 tablespoon wholemeal breadcrumbs*
- 1 egg, beaten
- 1 teaspoon olive oil*
- Fresh herbs (such as parsley and chives)
- Salt and pepper to taste

Using the measurements above will make exactly one serving of this meal. This serving size will match the nutritional information on this page.

Healthy Highlights:

WHOLE GRAIN | HEALTHY FATS | LEAN PROTEIN

Mackerel with Roasted Vegetables

NUTRITION INFORMATION

- Calories: 300
- Carbohydrates: 15g
- Protein: 25g
- Fats: 15g
- Sugar: 8g
- Sodium: 400mg

DIRECTIONS:

1. Preheat the air fryer to 180°C (356°F) for 3 minutes.
2. Toss the chopped vegetables with olive oil, mixed herbs, salt, and pepper.
3. Place the mackerel fillet and vegetables in the air fryer basket.
4. Cook for 12-15 minutes until the mackerel is cooked through and the vegetables are tender and slightly charred.
5. Serve hot with a squeeze of lemon juice.

INGREDIENTS

- 150g mackerel fillet*
- Assorted vegetables (such as bell peppers, zucchini, and cherry tomatoes), chopped
- 1 teaspoon olive oil*
- 1/2 teaspoon mixed herbs (like thyme, oregano, and basil)
- Salt and pepper to taste

Using the measurements above will make exactly one serving of this meal. This serving size will match the nutritional information on this page.

Healthy Highlights:

WHOLE GRAIN | HEALTHY FATS | LEAN PROTEIN

* *This recipe contains a healthy highlight that we don't recommend you switch with other ingredients*

84

Curried Cod

NUTRITION INFORMATION

- *Calories: 300*
- *Carbohydrates: 10g*
- *Protein: 30g*
- *Fats: 15g*
- *Sugar: 4g*
- *Sodium: 350mg*

DIRECTIONS:

1. Preheat the air fryer to 180°C (356°F) for 3 minutes.
2. Mix low-fat coconut milk, curry powder, turmeric, ground ginger, salt, and pepper to make a marinade.
3. Marinate the cod fillet in the mixture for 30 minutes.
4. Place the marinated cod in the air fryer basket and cook for 10-12 minutes until cooked through and lightly browned.
5. Garnish with fresh coriander before serving.

* This recipe contains a healthy highlight that we don't recommend you switch with other ingredients

INGREDIENTS

- *150g cod fillet**
- *1 tablespoon low-fat coconut milk*
- *1 teaspoon curry powder*
- *1/2 teaspoon turmeric*
- *1/2 teaspoon ground ginger*
- *Fresh coriander (cilantro) for garnish*
- *Salt and pepper to taste*

Using the measurements above will make exactly one serving of this meal. This serving size will match the nutritional information on this page.

Healthy Highlights:

WHOLE GRAIN | HEALTHY FATS | LEAN PROTEIN

Other Seafood Recipes

Explore a variety of seafood dishes that are tasty and suitable for diabetics using the air fryer.

Try air-fried Lemon and Thyme Seasoned Cockles, or a hearty protein-packed shrimp scampi. And for a beach-reminiscent treat, try air frying periwinkles with lemon garlic and serving with zucchini noodles. These recipes are sure to impress, so dive in and savour the flavours of the ocean!

Mussels with Garlic and Herbs

NUTRITION INFORMATION

- Calories: 250
- Carbohydrates: 12g
- Protein: 25g
- Fats: 12g
- Sugar: 2g
- Sodium: 450mg

DIRECTIONS:

1. Preheat the air fryer to 180°C (356°F) for 3 minutes.
2. In a bowl, mix the cleaned mussels with olive oil, minced garlic, chopped parsley, salt, and pepper.
3. Place the seasoned mussels in the air fryer basket.
4. Cook for 8-10 minutes until the mussels open up and are cooked through.
5. Serve hot with lemon wedges on the side.

INGREDIENTS

- 200g fresh mussels*, cleaned and debearded
- 1 tablespoon olive oil*
- 2 garlic cloves, minced
- 1 tablespoon fresh parsley, chopped
- Salt and pepper to taste
- Lemon wedges for serving

Using the measurements above will make exactly one serving of this meal. This serving size will match the nutritional information on this page.

Healthy Highlights:

WHOLE GRAIN | HEALTHY FATS | LEAN PROTEIN

* This recipe contains a healthy highlight that we don't recommend you switch with other ingredients

Basil and Tomato Mussels

NUTRITION INFORMATION

- Calories: 280
- Carbohydrates: 14g
- Protein: 27g
- Fats: 14g
- Sugar: 4g
- Sodium: 500mg

DIRECTIONS:

1. Preheat the air fryer to 180°C (356°F) for 3 minutes.
2. In a bowl, mix the cleaned mussels with olive oil, cherry tomatoes, basil, minced garlic, salt, and pepper.
3. Place the seasoned mussels in the air fryer basket.
4. Cook for 10-12 minutes until the mussels open up and are cooked through.
5. Serve hot, garnished with additional fresh basil if desired.

INGREDIENTS

- 200g fresh mussels*, cleaned and debearded
- 1 tablespoon olive oil*
- 1/2 cup cherry tomatoes, halved
- 2 tablespoons fresh basil, chopped
- 2 garlic cloves, minced
- Salt and pepper to taste

Using the measurements above will make exactly one serving of this meal. This serving size will match the nutritional information on this page.

Healthy Highlights:

WHOLE GRAIN | HEALTHY FATS | LEAN PROTEIN

* This recipe contains a healthy highlight that we don't recommend you switch with other ingredients

Lemon and Thyme Seasoned Cockles

NUTRITION INFORMATION

- ◆ *Calories: 220*
- ◆ *Carbohydrates: 10g*
- ◆ *Protein: 20g*
- ◆ *Fats: 10g*
- ◆ *Sugar: 1g*
- ◆ *Sodium: 400mg*

DIRECTIONS:

1. *Preheat the air fryer to 180°C (356°F) for 3 minutes.*
2. *In a bowl, mix the cleaned cockles with olive oil, lemon zest, fresh thyme leaves, salt, and pepper.*
3. *Place the seasoned cockles in the air fryer basket.*
4. *Cook for 6-8 minutes until the cockles are cooked through and tender.*
5. *Serve hot with a sprinkle of fresh lemon juice.*

* *This recipe contains a healthy highlight that we don't recommend you switch with other ingredients*

INGREDIENTS

- ◆ *200g fresh cockles*, cleaned*
- ◆ *1 tablespoon olive oil**
- ◆ *Zest of 1 lemon*
- ◆ *1 tablespoon fresh thyme leaves*
- ◆ *Salt and pepper to taste*

Using the measurements above will make exactly one serving of this meal. This serving size will match the nutritional information on this page.

Healthy Highlights:

WHOLE GRAIN — HEALTHY FATS — LEAN PROTEIN

Crab Cakes

NUTRITION INFORMATION
- *Calories: 300*
- *Carbohydrates: 10g*
- *Protein: 25g*
- *Fats: 18g*
- *Sugar: 2g*
- *Sodium: 450mg*

DIRECTIONS:
1. Preheat the air fryer to 180°C (356°F) for 3 minutes.
2. In a bowl, mix crab meat, breadcrumbs, beaten egg, Greek yogurt, Dijon mustard, Worcestershire sauce, chopped parsley, salt, and pepper.
3. Form the mixture into patties.
4. Lightly coat the crab cakes with olive oil.
5. Place the crab cakes in the air fryer basket.
6. Cook for 10-12 minutes until golden and crispy.
7. Serve hot with a side of salad or steamed vegetables.

* This recipe contains a healthy highlight that we don't recommend you switch with other ingredients

INGREDIENTS
- *150g crab meat*
- *1/4 cup wholemeal breadcrumbs**
- *1 egg, beaten*
- *1 tablespoon Greek yogurt**
- *1 teaspoon Dijon mustard*
- *1 teaspoon Worcestershire sauce*
- *1 tablespoon fresh parsley, chopped*
- *Salt and pepper to taste*
- *1 teaspoon olive oil* for coating*

Using the measurements above will make exactly one serving of this meal. This serving size will match the nutritional information on this page.

Healthy Highlights:

- WHOLE GRAIN
- HEALTHY FATS
- LEAN PROTEIN

Seafood Tacos

NUTRITION INFORMATION

- *Calories: 320*
- *Carbohydrates: 25g*
- *Protein: 28g*
- *Fats: 12g*
- *Sugar: 3g*
- *Sodium: 550mg*

DIRECTIONS:

1. Preheat the air fryer to 180°C (356°F) for 3 minutes.
2. Heat olive oil in a pan and cook the mixed seafood until done.
3. Warm the wholemeal tortillas in the air fryer for 1-2 minutes until slightly crispy.
4. Fill each tortilla with cooked seafood, shredded lettuce, diced tomatoes, diced onions, Greek yogurt, and chopped cilantro.
5. Serve immediately with lime wedges if desired.

INGREDIENTS

- 150g mixed seafood (shrimp, crab meat, etc.)*
- 2 small wholemeal tortillas*
- 1/2 cup shredded lettuce
- 1/4 cup diced tomatoes
- 1/4 cup diced onions
- 1/4 cup Greek yogurt* (as a healthy alternative to sour cream)
- 1 tablespoon fresh cilantro, chopped
- 1 teaspoon olive oil* for cooking

Using the measurements above will make exactly one serving of this meal. This serving size will match the nutritional information on this page.

Healthy Highlights:

- WHOLE GRAIN
- HEALTHY FATS
- LEAN PROTEIN

* This recipe contains a healthy highlight that we don't recommend you switch with other ingredients

Crab Meat Sandwich

NUTRITION INFORMATION
- Calories: 320
- Carbohydrates: 25g
- Protein: 30g
- Fats: 12g
- Sugar: 4g
- Sodium: 500mg

DIRECTIONS:
1. Preheat the air fryer to 180°C (356°F) for 3 minutes.
2. Mix crab meat, Greek yogurt, Dijon mustard, salt, and pepper in a bowl.
3. Lightly toast the wholemeal bread slices in the air fryer for 1-2 minutes.
4. Assemble the sandwich with the crab mixture, shredded lettuce, and sliced cucumber.
5. Drizzle a little olive oil on the sandwich.
6. Serve immediately with a side of salad or vegetable sticks.

INGREDIENTS
- 150g crab meat
- 2 slices wholemeal bread*
- 1 tablespoon Greek yogurt*
- 1 teaspoon Dijon mustard
- 1/4 cup shredded lettuce
- 1/4 cup sliced cucumber
- Salt and pepper to taste
- 1 teaspoon olive oil* for cooking

Using the measurements above will make exactly one serving of this meal. This serving size will match the nutritional information on this page.

Healthy Highlights:
- WHOLE GRAIN
- HEALTHY FATS
- LEAN PROTEIN

* This recipe contains a healthy highlight that we don't recommend you switch with other ingredients

Limpets with Herb Butter Shirataki Pasta

NUTRITION INFORMATION

- Calories: 280
- Carbohydrates: 10g
- Protein: 25g
- Fats: 15g
- Sugar: 2g
- Sodium: 400mg

DIRECTIONS:

1. Preheat the air fryer to 180°C (356°F) for 3 minutes.
2. In a pan, melt unsalted butter and add chopped parsley, garlic powder, salt, and pepper.
3. Add the cooked shirataki pasta to the pan and toss to coat with the herb butter mixture.
4. Place the limpets in the air fryer basket and cook for 8-10 minutes until cooked through.
5. Serve the herb butter pasta topped with cooked limpets.

*This recipe contains a healthy highlight that we don't recommend you switch with other ingredients

INGREDIENTS

- 200g cooked shirataki pasta (or any low-carb pasta substitute)
- 100g fresh limpets*
- 2 tablespoons unsalted butter
- 1 tablespoon fresh parsley, chopped
- 1/2 teaspoon garlic powder
- Salt and pepper to taste

Using the measurements above will make exactly one serving of this meal. This serving size will match the nutritional information on this page.

Healthy Highlights:

- WHOLE GRAIN
- HEALTHY FATS
- LEAN PROTEIN

Lemon Garlic Winkles & Zucchini Noodles

NUTRITION INFORMATION

- *Calories: 250*
- *Carbohydrates: 12g*
- *Protein: 20g*
- *Fats: 12g*
- *Sugar: 3g*
- *Sodium: 400mg*

DIRECTIONS:

1. Preheat the air fryer to 180°C (356°F) for 3 minutes.
2. In a pan, melt unsalted butter and add minced garlic, lemon zest, salt, and pepper.
3. Add the cleaned winkles to the pan and cook for 5-7 minutes until cooked through.
4. In the air fryer basket, place the zucchini noodles and cook for 3-4 minutes until slightly softened.
5. Toss the zucchini noodles with the cooked winkles and lemon garlic butter.
6. Garnish with fresh parsley before serving.

INGREDIENTS

- *150g winkles*, cleaned*
- *1 medium zucchini, spiralized into noodles*
- *2 tablespoons unsalted butter*
- *Zest of 1 lemon*
- *2 garlic cloves, minced*
- *Salt and pepper to taste*
- *Fresh parsley for garnish*

Using the measurements above will make exactly one serving of this meal. This serving size will match the nutritional information on this page.

Healthy Highlights:

WHOLE GRAIN | HEALTHY FATS | LEAN PROTEIN

* This recipe contains a healthy highlight that we don't recommend you switch with other ingredients

Shrimp Scampi

NUTRITION INFORMATION

- *Calories: 280*
- *Carbohydrates: 15g*
- *Protein: 25g*
- *Fats: 14g*
- *Sugar: 2g*
- *Sodium: 450mg*

DIRECTIONS:

1. Preheat the air fryer to 180°C (356°F) for 3 minutes.
2. In a pan, melt unsalted butter and olive oil over medium heat.
3. Add minced garlic and cook until fragrant.
4. Add shrimp to the pan and cook until pink and cooked through.
5. Stir in lemon zest, lemon juice, chopped parsley, salt, and pepper.
6. Place the cooked shrimp in the air fryer basket to keep warm while preparing other ingredients.
7. Serve the shrimp scampi hot with wholemeal bread if desired.

INGREDIENTS

- *150g shrimp*, peeled and deveined*
- *1 tablespoon unsalted butter*
- *1 tablespoon olive oil**
- *2 garlic cloves, minced*
- *Zest and juice of 1 lemon*
- *1 tablespoon fresh parsley, chopped*
- *Salt and pepper to taste*
- *Wholemeal bread* for serving (optional)*

Using the measurements above will make exactly one serving of this meal. This serving size will match the nutritional information on this page.

* This recipe contains a healthy highlight that we don't recommend you switch with other ingredients

Healthy Highlights:

- WHOLE GRAIN
- HEALTHY FATS
- LEAN PROTEIN

Crab Thermidor

NUTRITION INFORMATION

- *Calories: 350*
- *Carbohydrates: 20g*
- *Protein: 30g*
- *Fats: 18g*
- *Sugar: 4g*
- *Sodium: 550mg*

DIRECTIONS:

1. Preheat the air fryer to 180°C (356°F) for 3 minutes.
2. In a pan, melt unsalted butter over medium heat.
3. Stir in plain flour to make a roux.
4. Gradually add low-fat milk, stirring constantly until thickened.
5. Stir in grated Parmesan cheese, Dijon mustard, chopped parsley, salt, and pepper.
6. Fold in crab meat gently until well combined.
7. Place the crab Thermidor mixture in a baking dish and cook in the air fryer for 10-12 minutes until bubbly and golden on top.
8. Serve hot as a main dish.

INGREDIENTS

- *150g crab meat**
- *1 tablespoon unsalted butter*
- *1 tablespoon plain flour*
- *1/2 cup low-fat milk*
- *1/4 cup grated Parmesan cheese*
- *1 teaspoon Dijon mustard*
- *1 tablespoon fresh parsley, chopped*
- *Salt and pepper to taste*

Using the measurements above will make exactly one serving of this meal. This serving size will match the nutritional information on this page.

Healthy Highlights:

WHOLE GRAIN | HEALTHY FATS | LEAN PROTEIN

* This recipe contains a healthy highlight that we don't recommend you switch with other ingredients

Vegetarian Recipes

Delight in a range of vegetarian recipes that are diabetes-friendly and made in the air fryer.

Enjoy crispy air-fried brussel sprouts with balsamic glaze or stuffed portobello mushroom caps with quinoa and kale. You can also prepare air-fried chestnut mushroom pie. These recipes are a veggie lover's dream, so get cooking and relish the vibrant tastes!

Cauliflower Steaks

NUTRITION INFORMATION

- *Calories: 200*
- *Carbohydrates: 15g*
- *Protein: 8g*
- *Fats: 12g*
- *Sugar: 5g*
- *Sodium: 350mg*

DIRECTIONS:

1. Preheat the air fryer to 200°C (392°F) for 3 minutes.
2. Slice the cauliflower into thick "steaks" about 1 inch thick.
3. In a bowl, mix olive oil, garlic powder, smoked paprika, salt, and pepper.
4. Brush both sides of the cauliflower steaks with the oil mixture.
5. Place the cauliflower steaks in the air fryer basket.
6. Cook for 12-15 minutes until golden and tender, flipping halfway through cooking.
7. Garnish with fresh parsley before serving.

INGREDIENTS

- *1 medium cauliflower head*
- *1 tablespoon olive oil**
- *1 teaspoon garlic powder*
- *1 teaspoon smoked paprika*
- *Salt and pepper to taste*
- *Fresh parsley for garnish*

Using the measurements above will make exactly one serving of this meal. This serving size will match the nutritional information on this page.

Healthy Highlights:

WHOLE GRAIN | HEALTHY FATS | LEAN PROTEIN

* This recipe contains a healthy highlight that we don't recommend you switch with other ingredients

Brussels Sprouts with Balsamic Glaze

NUTRITION INFORMATION

- *Calories: 180*
- *Carbohydrates: 20g*
- *Protein: 5g*
- *Fats: 10g*
- *Sugar: 8g*
- *Sodium: 250mg*

DIRECTIONS:

1. Preheat the air fryer to 200°C (392°F) for 3 minutes.
2. Toss Brussels sprouts with olive oil, balsamic vinegar, honey (if using), salt, and pepper in a bowl.
3. Place the Brussels sprouts in the air fryer basket.
4. Cook for 10-12 minutes until caramelized and tender, shaking the basket halfway through cooking.
5. Serve hot as a side dish.

* *This recipe contains a healthy highlight that we don't recommend you switch with other ingredients*

INGREDIENTS

- *150g Brussels sprouts, trimmed and halved*
- *1 tablespoon olive oil**
- *1 tablespoon balsamic vinegar*
- *1 teaspoon honey (optional for sweetness)*
- *Salt and pepper to taste*

Using the measurements above will make exactly one serving of this meal. This serving size will match the nutritional information on this page.

Healthy Highlights:

WHOLE GRAIN | HEALTHY FATS | LEAN PROTEIN

Asparagus with Lemon and Parmesan

NUTRITION INFORMATION
- *Calories: 150*
- *Carbohydrates: 10g*
- *Protein: 8g*
- *Fats: 10g*
- *Sugar: 4g*
- *Sodium: 300mg*

DIRECTIONS:
1. Preheat the air fryer to 200°C (392°F) for 3 minutes.
2. Toss asparagus spears with olive oil, lemon zest, grated Parmesan, salt, and pepper in a bowl.
3. Place the asparagus in the air fryer basket.
4. Cook for 8-10 minutes until tender and lightly charred, shaking the basket halfway through cooking.
5. Serve hot, garnished with a sprinkle of additional Parmesan cheese if desired.

INGREDIENTS
- *150g asparagus spears, trimmed*
- *1 tablespoon olive oil**
- *Zest of 1 lemon*
- *1 tablespoon grated Parmesan cheese*
- *Salt and pepper to taste*

Using the measurements above will make exactly one serving of this meal. This serving size will match the nutritional information on this page.

Healthy Highlights:
- WHOLE GRAIN
- HEALTHY FATS
- LEAN PROTEIN

* This recipe contains a healthy highlight that we don't recommend you switch with other ingredients

Chickpea Patties

NUTRITION INFORMATION

- Calories: 250
- Carbohydrates: 20g
- Protein: 10g
- Fats: 14g
- Sugar: 2g
- Sodium: 400mg

DIRECTIONS:

1. Preheat the air fryer to 180°C (356°F) for 3 minutes.
2. Mash the cooked chickpeas in a bowl.
3. Add breadcrumbs, ground cumin, paprika, garlic powder, salt, and pepper to the mashed chickpeas. Mix well to form a dough-like mixture.
4. Shape the mixture into patties.
5. Brush the patties with olive oil.
6. Place the chickpea patties in the air fryer basket.
7. Cook for 12-15 minutes until golden and crispy, flipping halfway through cooking.
8. Serve hot with a side salad or in a wholemeal bun for a burger.

* This recipe contains a healthy highlight that we don't recommend you switch with other ingredients

INGREDIENTS

- 1 cup cooked chickpeas
- 1/4 cup breadcrumbs*
- 1/2 teaspoon ground cumin
- 1/2 teaspoon paprika
- 1/4 teaspoon garlic powder
- Salt and pepper to taste
- 1 tablespoon olive oil* for cooking

Using the measurements above will make exactly one serving of this meal. This serving size will match the nutritional information on this page.

Healthy Highlights:

- WHOLE GRAIN
- HEALTHY FATS
- LEAN PROTEIN

Sweet Potato and Black Bean Tacos

NUTRITION INFORMATION

- *Calories: 300*
- *Carbohydrates: 35g*
- *Protein: 8g*
- *Fats: 12g*
- *Sugar: 6g*
- *Sodium: 400mg*

DIRECTIONS:

1. Preheat the air fryer to 200°C (392°F) for 3 minutes.
2. Toss diced sweet potato with olive oil, ground cumin, paprika, salt, and pepper.
3. Spread the sweet potato cubes evenly in the air fryer basket.
4. Cook for 15-18 minutes until tender and slightly crispy, shaking the basket halfway through cooking.
5. Warm the wholemeal tortillas in the air fryer for 1-2 minutes.
6. Fill each tortilla with cooked sweet potato cubes, black beans, and optional toppings.
7. Serve hot as tacos.

INGREDIENTS

- *2 small wholemeal tortillas**
- *1 medium sweet potato, peeled and diced*
- *1/2 cup cooked black beans*
- *1/2 teaspoon ground cumin*
- *1/2 teaspoon paprika*
- *Salt and pepper to taste*
- *1 tablespoon olive oil**
- *Optional toppings: diced tomatoes, avocado slices, Greek yogurt*

Using the measurements above will make exactly one serving of this meal. This serving size will match the nutritional information on this page.

Healthy Highlights:

WHOLE GRAIN | HEALTHY FATS | LEAN PROTEIN

* This recipe contains a healthy highlight that we don't recommend you switch with other ingredients

Chestnut Mushroom Pie

NUTRITION INFORMATION

- Calories: 320
- Carbohydrates: 30g
- Protein: 12g
- Fats: 18g
- Sugar: 5g
- Sodium: 400mg

DIRECTIONS:

1. Preheat the air fryer to 200°C (392°F) for 3 minutes.
2. Remove the stems from Portobello mushroom caps and gently scrape out the gills.
3. In a pan, heat olive oil and sauté minced garlic until fragrant.
4. Add chopped kale and cook until wilted.
5. Stir in cooked quinoa and season with salt and pepper.
6. Fill the mushroom caps with the quinoa-kale mixture.
7. Place the stuffed mushroom caps in the air fryer basket.
8. Cook for 10-12 minutes until the mushrooms are tender and the filling is heated through.
9. Optionally, sprinkle with grated Parmesan cheese before serving.

*This recipe contains a healthy highlight that we don't recommend you switch with other ingredients

INGREDIENTS

- 2 large Portobello mushroom caps
- 1/2 cup cooked quinoa
- 1 cup chopped kale
- 1 clove garlic, minced
- 1 tablespoon olive oil*
- Salt and pepper to taste
- Grated Parmesan cheese (optional)

Using the measurements above will make exactly one serving of this meal. This serving size will match the nutritional information on this page.

Healthy Highlights:

WHOLE GRAIN | HEALTHY FATS | LEAN PROTEIN

Portobello Mushroom Caps with Quinoa and Kale

NUTRITION INFORMATION

- *Calories: 320*
- *Carbohydrates: 30g*
- *Protein: 12g*
- *Fats: 18g*
- *Sugar: 5g*
- *Sodium: 400mg*

DIRECTIONS:

1. Preheat the air fryer to 200°C (392°F) for 3 minutes.
2. Remove the stems from Portobello mushroom caps and gently scrape out the gills.
3. In a pan, heat olive oil and sauté minced garlic until fragrant.
4. Add chopped kale and cook until wilted.
5. Stir in cooked quinoa and season with salt and pepper.
6. Fill the mushroom caps with the quinoa-kale mixture.
7. Place the stuffed mushroom caps in the air fryer basket.
8. Cook for 10-12 minutes until the mushrooms are tender and the filling is heated through.
9. Optionally, sprinkle with grated Parmesan cheese before serving.

* This recipe contains a healthy highlight that we don't recommend you switch with other ingredients

INGREDIENTS

- *2 large Portobello mushroom caps*
- *1/2 cup cooked quinoa*
- *1 cup chopped kale*
- *1 clove garlic, minced*
- *1 tablespoon olive oil**
- *Salt and pepper to taste*
- *Grated Parmesan cheese (optional)*

Using the measurements above will make exactly one serving of this meal. This serving size will match the nutritional information on this page.

Healthy Highlights:

- WHOLE GRAIN
- HEALTHY FATS
- LEAN PROTEIN

104

Cauliflower and Almond Fritters

NUTRITION INFORMATION

- Calories: 280
- Carbohydrates: 20g
- Protein: 10g
- Fats: 18g
- Sugar: 4g
- Sodium: 350mg

DIRECTIONS:

1. Preheat the air fryer to 180°C (356°F) for 3 minutes.
2. In a bowl, combine mashed cauliflower, almond meal, beaten egg, chopped coriander, ground cumin, salt, and pepper to form a thick batter.
3. Heat olive oil in a pan over medium heat.
4. Spoon the cauliflower batter into the pan to form fritters.
5. Cook for 3-4 minutes per side until golden and crispy.
6. Place the cooked fritters in the air fryer basket to keep warm while cooking the remaining batches.
7. Serve hot as a delicious and nutritious snack or side dish.

* This recipe contains a healthy highlight that we don't recommend you switch with other ingredients

INGREDIENTS

- 1 cup cauliflower florets, steamed and mashed
- 1/4 cup almond meal*
- 1 egg, beaten
- 1 tablespoon chopped fresh coriander (cilantro)
- 1/2 teaspoon ground cumin
- Salt and pepper to taste
- 1 tablespoon olive oil* for cooking

Using the measurements above will make exactly one serving of this meal. This serving size will match the nutritional information on this page.

Healthy Highlights:

WHOLE GRAIN | HEALTHY FATS | LEAN PROTEIN

Zucchini and Lentil Stuffed Tomatoes

NUTRITION INFORMATION

- Calories: 280
- Carbohydrates: 35g
- Protein: 10g
- Fats: 12g
- Sugar: 8g
- Sodium: 400mg

DIRECTIONS:

1. Preheat the air fryer to 180°C (356°F) for 3 minutes.
2. Cut the tops off the tomatoes and scoop out the flesh, leaving a shell. Reserve the flesh for the filling.
3. Heat olive oil in a pan and sauté onion and garlic until softened.
4. Add diced zucchini and reserved tomato flesh. Cook until vegetables are tender.
5. Stir in cooked lentils, tomato paste, dried oregano, salt, and pepper. Cook for another 2-3 minutes.
6. Stuff the tomato shells with the lentil-zucchini mixture.
7. Place the stuffed tomatoes in the air fryer basket.
8. Cook for 10-12 minutes until the tomatoes are softened and the filling is heated through.
9. Optionally, sprinkle grated cheese on top before serving for added flavour.

* This recipe contains a healthy highlight that we don't recommend you switch with other ingredients

INGREDIENTS

- 2 large tomatoes
- 1/2 cup cooked lentils
- 1 small zucchini, diced
- 1/2 onion, finely chopped
- 1 clove garlic, minced
- 1 tablespoon olive oil*
- 1 tablespoon tomato paste
- 1 teaspoon dried oregano
- Salt and pepper to taste
- Grated cheese (optional)

Using the measurements above will make exactly one serving of this meal. This serving size will match the nutritional information on this page.

Healthy Highlights:

- WHOLE GRAIN
- HEALTHY FATS
- LEAN PROTEIN

Stuffed Eggplant with Quinoa and Spinach

NUTRITION INFORMATION

- Calories: 320
- Carbohydrates: 40g
- Protein: 12g
- Fats: 14g
- Sugar: 6g
- Sodium: 450mg

DIRECTIONS:

1. Preheat the air fryer to 200°C (392°F) for 3 minutes.
2. Cut the eggplant in half lengthwise and scoop out the flesh, leaving a shell. Chop the scooped-out flesh.
3. Heat olive oil in a pan and sauté onion and garlic until translucent.
4. Add chopped eggplant flesh and cook until softened.
5. Stir in cooked quinoa, chopped spinach, dried thyme, salt, and pepper. Cook until spinach wilts.
6. Stuff the eggplant halves with the quinoa-spinach mixture.
7. Place the stuffed eggplants in the air fryer basket.
8. Cook for 15-18 minutes until the eggplants are tender and the filling is heated through.
9. Optionally, sprinkle grated cheese on top before serving for added richness.

* This recipe contains a healthy highlight that we don't recommend you switch with other ingredients

INGREDIENTS

- 1 medium eggplant
- 1/2 cup cooked quinoa
- 1 cup fresh spinach, chopped
- 1/2 onion, finely chopped
- 1 clove garlic, minced
- 1 tablespoon olive oil*
- 1/4 teaspoon dried thyme
- Salt and pepper to taste
- Grated cheese (optional)

Using the measurements above will make exactly one serving of this meal. This serving size will match the nutritional information on this page.

Healthy Highlights:

WHOLE GRAIN | HEALTHY FATS | LEAN PROTEIN

Snacks

Satisfy your cravings with healthy, diabetic-friendly snacks made in the air fryer.

Imagine crunchy kale crisps seasoned with sea salt, or spiced chickpeas for a protein-packed treat. Air-fried cheesy spinach balls are a delicious, low-glycaemic snack option. These snacks are perfect for any time, so get snacking and enjoy guilt-free nibbles!

Sweet Potato Skins

NUTRITION INFORMATION

- Calories: 220
- Carbohydrates: 25g
- Protein: 5g
- Fats: 12g
- Sugar: 5g
- Sodium: 300mg

DIRECTIONS:

1. Preheat the air fryer to 200°C (392°F) for 3 minutes.
2. Wash and scrub sweet potatoes. Pat dry.
3. Cut sweet potatoes lengthwise into halves.
4. Scoop out some flesh from each half to create a hollow space for the filling.
5. Brush sweet potato skins with olive oil and sprinkle with salt and pepper.
6. Place the sweet potato skins in the air fryer basket.
7. Cook for 12-15 minutes until skins are crispy and insides are tender.
8. Fill each skin with optional toppings like grated cheese, Greek yogurt, and chopped chives before serving.

*This recipe contains a healthy highlight that we don't recommend you switch with other ingredients

INGREDIENTS

- 2 medium sweet potatoes
- 1 tablespoon olive oil*
- Salt and pepper to taste
- Optional toppings: grated cheese, Greek yogurt, chopped chives

Using the measurements above will make exactly one serving of this meal. This serving size will match the nutritional information on this page.

Healthy Highlights:

WHOLE GRAIN | HEALTHY FATS | LEAN PROTEIN

Kale Chips

NUTRITION INFORMATION

- *Calories: 50*
- *Carbohydrates: 8g*
- *Protein: 3g*
- *Fats: 2g*
- *Sugar: 1g*
- *Sodium: 100mg*

DIRECTIONS:

1. Preheat the air fryer to 160°C (320°F) for 3 minutes.
2. In a bowl, massage kale leaves with olive oil until coated evenly.
3. Season with salt, pepper, and optional seasonings as desired.
4. Place the kale leaves in the air fryer basket in a single layer.
5. Cook for 6-8 minutes until kale becomes crispy, shaking the basket halfway through cooking.
6. Remove from the air fryer and let cool before serving.

INGREDIENTS

- 2 cups kale leaves, stems removed and torn into pieces
- 1 tablespoon olive oil*
- Salt and pepper to taste
- Optional seasonings: nutritional yeast, garlic powder, paprika

Using the measurements above will make exactly one serving of this meal. This serving size will match the nutritional information on this page.

Healthy Highlights:

WHOLE GRAIN | HEALTHY FATS | LEAN PROTEIN

* This recipe contains a healthy highlight that we don't recommend you switch with other ingredients

Zucchini Fries

NUTRITION INFORMATION
- *Calories: 150*
- *Carbohydrates: 15g*
- *Protein: 5g*
- *Fats: 8g*
- *Sugar: 3g*
- *Sodium: 250mg*

DIRECTIONS:
1. Preheat the air fryer to 200°C (392°F) for 3 minutes.
2. In a bowl, mix wholemeal breadcrumbs, grated Parmesan cheese, Italian seasoning, salt, and pepper.
3. Dip zucchini sticks into beaten egg, then coat with the breadcrumb mixture.
4. Place the coated zucchini sticks in the air fryer basket.
5. Lightly coat with cooking spray or olive oil.
6. Cook for 10-12 minutes until golden and crispy, flipping halfway through cooking.
7. Serve hot with a dipping sauce of your choice.

* This recipe contains a healthy highlight that we don't recommend you switch with other ingredients

INGREDIENTS
- 1 medium zucchini, cut into sticks
- 1/4 cup wholemeal breadcrumbs*
- 1/4 cup grated Parmesan cheese
- 1 teaspoon Italian seasoning
- Salt and pepper to taste
- 1 egg, beaten
- Cooking spray or olive oil* for coating

Using the measurements above will make exactly one serving of this meal. This serving size will match the nutritional information on this page.

Healthy Highlights:

WHOLE GRAIN | HEALTHY FATS | LEAN PROTEIN

Broccoli Tots

NUTRITION INFORMATION

- Calories: 120
- Carbohydrates: 10g
- Protein: 6g
- Fats: 6g
- Sugar: 2g
- Sodium: 200mg

DIRECTIONS:

1. Preheat the air fryer to 200°C (392°F) for 3 minutes.
2. In a bowl, mix chopped cooked broccoli, wholemeal breadcrumbs, grated Cheddar cheese, beaten egg, garlic powder, salt, and pepper.
3. Shape the mixture into tots or small cylinders.
4. Lightly coat the tots with cooking spray or olive oil.
5. Place the broccoli tots in the air fryer basket.
6. Cook for 10-12 minutes until golden and crispy.
7. Serve hot with a dipping sauce or as a side dish.

INGREDIENTS

- 1 cup cooked broccoli, finely chopped
- 1/4 cup wholemeal breadcrumbs*
- 1/4 cup grated Cheddar cheese
- 1 egg, beaten
- 1/2 teaspoon garlic powder
- Salt and pepper to taste
- Cooking spray or olive oil* for coating

Using the measurements above will make exactly one serving of this meal. This serving size will match the nutritional information on this page.

Healthy Highlights:

- WHOLE GRAIN
- HEALTHY FATS
- LEAN PROTEIN

* This recipe contains a healthy highlight that we don't recommend you switch with other ingredients

Parmesan Eggplant Fries

NUTRITION INFORMATION
- Calories: 180
- Carbohydrates: 15g
- Protein: 8g
- Fats: 10g
- Sugar: 4g
- Sodium: 300mg

DIRECTIONS:
1. Preheat the air fryer to 200°C (392°F) for 3 minutes.
2. In a bowl, mix wholemeal breadcrumbs, grated Parmesan cheese, Italian seasoning, salt, and pepper.
3. Dip eggplant fries into beaten egg, then coat with the breadcrumb mixture.
4. Place the coated eggplant fries in the air fryer basket.
5. Lightly coat with cooking spray or olive oil.
6. Cook for 10-12 minutes until golden and crispy, flipping halfway through cooking.
7. Serve hot with a dipping sauce of your choice.

INGREDIENTS
- 1 small eggplant, cut into fries
- 1/4 cup wholemeal breadcrumbs*
- 1/4 cup grated Parmesan cheese
- 1 egg, beaten
- 1/2 teaspoon Italian seasoning
- Salt and pepper to taste
- Cooking spray or olive oil* for coating

Using the measurements above will make exactly one serving of this meal. This serving size will match the nutritional information on this page.

Healthy Highlights:
- WHOLE GRAIN
- HEALTHY FATS
- LEAN PROTEIN

* This recipe contains a healthy highlight that we don't recommend you switch with other ingredients

Courgette Fritters

NUTRITION INFORMATION

- *Calories: 160*
- *Carbohydrates: 12g*
- *Protein: 6g*
- *Fats: 10g*
- *Sugar: 2g*
- *Sodium: 250mg*

DIRECTIONS:

1. Preheat the air fryer to 180°C (356°F) for 3 minutes.
2. In a bowl, combine grated courgette, wholemeal flour, grated Parmesan cheese, beaten egg, chopped fresh herbs, salt, and pepper.
3. Mix until well combined to form a batter.
4. Lightly coat the air fryer basket with cooking spray or olive oil.
5. Spoon the courgette batter into the air fryer in small fritter shapes.
6. Cook for 10-12 minutes until fritters are golden and crispy, flipping halfway through cooking.
7. Serve hot as a snack or side dish.

* This recipe contains a healthy highlight that we don't recommend you switch with other ingredients

INGREDIENTS

- *1 medium courgette, grated and excess water squeezed out*
- *1/4 cup wholemeal flour**
- *1/4 cup grated Parmesan cheese*
- *1 egg, beaten*
- *1 tablespoon chopped fresh herbs (such as parsley or chives)*
- *Salt and pepper to taste*
- *Cooking spray or olive oil* for cooking*

Using the measurements above will make exactly one serving of this meal. This serving size will match the nutritional information on this page.

Healthy Highlights:

- WHOLE GRAIN
- HEALTHY FATS
- LEAN PROTEIN

Cheesy Spinach Balls

NUTRITION INFORMATION

- *Calories: 180*
- *Carbohydrates: 8g*
- *Protein: 12g*
- *Fats: 10g*
- *Sugar: 2g*
- *Sodium: 300mg*

DIRECTIONS:

1. Preheat the air fryer to 180°C (356°F) for 3 minutes.
2. In a bowl, mix chopped fresh spinach, grated Cheddar cheese, wholemeal breadcrumbs, beaten egg, garlic powder, salt, and pepper.
3. Shape the mixture into small balls.
4. Lightly coat the air fryer basket with cooking spray or olive oil.
5. Place the spinach balls in the air fryer basket.
6. Cook for 8-10 minutes until golden and firm, shaking the basket halfway through cooking.
7. Serve hot as a snack or appetiser.

INGREDIENTS

- 1 cup chopped fresh spinach
- 1/2 cup grated Cheddar cheese
- 1/4 cup wholemeal breadcrumbs*
- 1 egg, beaten
- 1/2 teaspoon garlic powder
- Salt and pepper to taste
- Cooking spray or olive oil* for cooking

Using the measurements above will make exactly one serving of this meal. This serving size will match the nutritional information on this page.

Healthy Highlights:

WHOLE GRAIN | HEALTHY FATS | LEAN PROTEIN

* This recipe contains a healthy highlight that we don't recommend you switch with other ingredients

Chickpea Snacks

NUTRITION INFORMATION
- *Calories: 160*
- *Carbohydrates: 20g*
- *Protein: 8g*
- *Fats: 6g*
- *Sugar: 3g*
- *Sodium: 250mg*

DIRECTIONS:
1. Preheat the air fryer to 180°C (356°F) for 3 minutes.
2. In a bowl, toss cooked chickpeas with olive oil, smoked paprika, garlic powder, salt, and pepper until coated.
3. Place the seasoned chickpeas in the air fryer basket.
4. Cook for 15-18 minutes until crispy, shaking the basket halfway through cooking.
5. Remove from the air fryer and let cool slightly before serving as a crunchy snack.

INGREDIENTS
- 1 cup cooked chickpeas, drained and rinsed
- 1 tablespoon olive oil*
- 1 teaspoon smoked paprika
- 1/2 teaspoon garlic powder
- Salt and pepper to taste

Using the measurements above will make exactly one serving of this meal. This serving size will match the nutritional information on this page.

Healthy Highlights:
- WHOLE GRAIN
- HEALTHY FATS
- LEAN PROTEIN

* This recipe contains a healthy highlight that we don't recommend you switch with other ingredients

Chicken Strips with Herbed Yogurt Dip

NUTRITION INFORMATION

- ◆ *Calories: 280*
- ◆ *Carbohydrates: 15g*
- ◆ *Protein: 30g*
- ◆ *Fats: 10g*
- ◆ *Sugar: 3g*
- ◆ *Sodium: 400mg*

DIRECTIONS:

1. Preheat the air fryer to 200°C (392°F) for 3 minutes.
2. In a bowl, mix wholemeal breadcrumbs, grated Parmesan cheese, dried mixed herbs, salt, and pepper.
3. Dip chicken strips into beaten egg, then coat with the breadcrumb mixture.
4. Lightly coat the air fryer basket with cooking spray or olive oil.
5. Place the coated chicken strips in the air fryer basket.
6. Cook for 12-15 minutes until chicken is cooked through and coating is crispy, flipping halfway through cooking.
7. Meanwhile, prepare the herbed yogurt dip by combining Greek yogurt, chopped fresh herbs, lemon juice, salt, and pepper in a bowl.
8. Serve the chicken strips hot with the herbed yogurt dip on the side.

* *This recipe contains a healthy highlight that we don't recommend you switch with other ingredients*

INGREDIENTS

- ◆ *1 boneless, skinless chicken breast, cut into strips*
- ◆ *1/4 cup wholemeal breadcrumbs**
- ◆ *1/4 cup grated Parmesan cheese*
- ◆ *1 egg, beaten*
- ◆ *1 teaspoon dried mixed herbs (such as oregano, basil, thyme)*
- ◆ *Salt and pepper to taste*
- ◆ *Cooking spray or olive oil* for coating*

Using the measurements above will make exactly one serving of this meal. This serving size will match the nutritional information on this page.

Healthy Highlights:

WHOLE GRAIN | HEALTHY FATS | LEAN PROTEIN

Bacon-Wrapped Asparagus

NUTRITION INFORMATION

- *Calories: 200*
- *Carbohydrates: 8g*
- *Protein: 10g*
- *Fats: 15g*
- *Sugar: 2g*
- *Sodium: 350mg*

DIRECTIONS:

1. Preheat the air fryer to 200°C (392°F) for 3 minutes.
2. Season asparagus spears with salt, pepper, and olive oil (if using).
3. Wrap each asparagus spear with a slice of lean bacon.
4. Place the bacon-wrapped asparagus in the air fryer basket.
5. Cook for 10-12 minutes until bacon is crispy and asparagus is tender.
6. Serve hot as a delicious appetizer or side dish.

INGREDIENTS

- *8-10 asparagus spears, trimmed*
- *4 slices lean bacon*
- *1 tablespoon olive oil* (optional)*
- *Salt and pepper to taste*

Using the measurements above will make exactly one serving of this meal. This serving size will match the nutritional information on this page.

Healthy Highlights:

WHOLE GRAIN | HEALTHY FATS | LEAN PROTEIN

* *This recipe contains a healthy highlight that we don't recommend you switch with other ingredients*

Desserts

Indulge in sweet treats that won't derail your diabetic meal plan with air fryer desserts.

Picture low-carb apple crumble made with coconut flour crust, or a batch of air-fried chocolate cupcakes made with almond flour and chocolate nibs. For a sweet and sour fix, try air-fried lemon chia seed cake with sweet stevia glaze, satisfying and low in sugar. These desserts are the perfect end to any meal, so get baking and enjoy a sweet finish!

Date and Almond Cake with Sugar-Free Toffee Sauce

NUTRITION INFORMATION

- *Calories: 250*
- *Carbohydrates: 30g*
- *Protein: 5g*
- *Fats: 12g*
- *Sugar: 10g*
- *Sodium: 150mg*

DIRECTIONS:

1. Preheat the air fryer to 160°C (320°F) for 3 minutes.
2. In a mixing bowl, combine almond flour, chopped dates, egg, almond milk, olive oil (if using), baking powder, vanilla extract, and a pinch of salt. Mix until well combined.
3. Pour the batter into a small greased cake tin or ramekin.
4. Place the cake tin in the air fryer basket.
5. Cook for 20-25 minutes until the cake is firm and golden on top.
6. Let the cake cool slightly before serving.
7. Drizzle with sugar-free toffee sauce if desired.

INGREDIENTS

- 1/2 cup almond flour*
- 1/4 cup chopped dates
- 1 egg
- 2 tablespoons unsweetened almond milk
- 1 tablespoon olive oil* (optional)
- 1/2 teaspoon baking powder
- 1/4 teaspoon vanilla extract
- Pinch of salt
- Sugar-free toffee sauce for topping (optional)

Using the measurements above will make exactly one serving of this meal. This serving size will match the nutritional information on this page.

Healthy Highlights:

WHOLE GRAIN | HEALTHY FATS | LEAN PROTEIN

* This recipe contains a healthy highlight that we don't recommend you switch with other ingredients

120

Almond Flour Chocolate Cupcake

NUTRITION INFORMATION

- Calories: 200
- Carbohydrates: 11g
- Protein: 7g
- Fats: 15g
- Sugar: 5g
- Sodium: 100mg

DIRECTIONS:

1. Preheat the air fryer to 160°C (320°F) for 3 minutes.
2. In a bowl, mix the almond flour, unsweetened cocoa powder, baking powder, sugar-free sweetener, and a pinch of salt.
3. In a separate bowl, whisk the egg, melted coconut oil, and vanilla extract until well combined.
4. Add the wet ingredients to the dry ingredients and mix until a smooth batter forms. Fold in the cacao nibs.
5. Lightly grease a small oven-safe ramekin or silicone cupcake mould with cooking spray or olive oil.
6. Pour the batter into the prepared ramekin or mould. Place the ramekin or mould in the air fryer basket.
7. Cook for 10-12 minutes, or until a toothpick inserted into the centre of the cupcake comes out clean.
8. Let the cupcake cool slightly before removing it from the ramekin or mould.
9. Serve and enjoy your delicious and healthy almond flour chocolate cupcake with cacao nibs.

* This recipe contains a healthy highlight that we don't recommend you switch with other ingredients

INGREDIENTS

- 1/4 cup almond flour*
- 1 tablespoon unsweetened cocoa powder
- 1/4 teaspoon baking powder
- 1 large egg
- 1 tablespoon coconut oil* (melted)
- 1 tablespoon sugar-free sweetener (such as erythritol or stevia)
- 1/4 teaspoon vanilla extract
- 1 tablespoon cacao nibs
- A pinch of salt

Using the measurements above will make exactly one serving of this meal. This serving size will match the nutritional information on this page.

Healthy Highlights:

WHOLE GRAIN | HEALTHY FATS | LEAN PROTEIN

Sugar-Free Banana and Avocado Pie with Almond Crust

NUTRITION INFORMATION

- *Calories: 280*
- *Carbohydrates: 25g*
- *Protein: 6g*
- *Fats: 18g*
- *Sugar: 5g*
- *Sodium: 200mg*

DIRECTIONS:

1. Preheat the air fryer to 160°C (320°F) for 3 minutes.
2. In a bowl, combine mashed banana, mashed avocado, almond flour, melted coconut oil, almond milk, vanilla extract, and a pinch of salt. Mix until a dough forms.
3. Press the dough into a small greased pie dish or ramekin to form the crust.
4. Place the pie dish in the air fryer basket.
5. Cook for 15-18 minutes until the crust is golden and firm.
6. Let the crust cool completely before filling.
7. Fill the crust with your favourite sugar-free pie filling or topping.

INGREDIENTS

- 1/2 ripe banana, mashed
- 1/2 ripe avocado, mashed
- 1/4 cup almond flour*
- 1 tablespoon coconut oil, melted
- 1 tablespoon unsweetened almond milk
- 1/2 teaspoon vanilla extract
- Pinch of salt

Using the measurements above will make exactly one serving of this meal. This serving size will match the nutritional information on this page.

Healthy Highlights:

- WHOLE GRAIN
- HEALTHY FATS
- LEAN PROTEIN

* *This recipe contains a healthy highlight that we don't recommend you switch with other ingredients*

Low-Carb Apple Crumble with Coconut Flour Crust

NUTRITION INFORMATION

- *Calories: 220*
- *Carbohydrates: 15g*
- *Protein: 5g*
- *Fats: 16g*
- *Sugar: 5g*
- *Sodium: 150mg*

DIRECTIONS:

1. Preheat the air fryer to 160°C (320°F) for 3 minutes.
2. In a bowl, mix diced apple with cinnamon and sugar-free sweetener if using.
3. In another bowl, combine coconut flour, almond flour, shredded coconut, melted coconut oil, and a pinch of salt to make the crumble topping.
4. Place the diced apple mixture in a small greased baking dish or ramekin.
5. Sprinkle the crumble topping evenly over the apples.
6. Place the baking dish in the air fryer basket.
7. Cook for 15-18 minutes until the topping is golden and the apples are tender.
8. Serve warm with a dollop of sugar-free whipped cream or Greek yogurt if desired.

INGREDIENTS

- 1 small apple, peeled and diced
- 1 tablespoon coconut flour*
- 1 tablespoon almond flour*
- 1 tablespoon unsweetened shredded coconut
- 1 tablespoon coconut oil, melted
- 1/2 teaspoon cinnamon
- Pinch of salt
- Sugar-free sweetener to taste (optional)

Using the measurements above will make exactly one serving of this meal. This serving size will match the nutritional information on this page.

Healthy Highlights:

WHOLE GRAIN | HEALTHY FATS | LEAN PROTEIN

* This recipe contains a healthy highlight that we don't recommend you switch with other ingredients

Victoria Sponge Cake with Raspberry Chia Jam

NUTRITION INFORMATION

- *Calories: 280*
- *Carbohydrates: 25g*
- *Protein: 6g*
- *Fats: 18g*
- *Sugar: 8g*
- *Sodium: 200mg*

DIRECTIONS:

1. Preheat the air fryer to 160°C (320°F) for 3 minutes.
2. In a mixing bowl, whisk together almond flour, coconut flour, unsweetened applesauce, eggs, almond milk, baking powder, and vanilla extract until smooth.
3. Pour the batter into a greased small cake tin or ramekin.
4. Place the cake tin in the air fryer basket.
5. Cook for 20-25 minutes until the cake is golden and a toothpick inserted into the centre comes out clean.
6. Let the cake cool completely before slicing horizontally and spreading sugar-free raspberry chia jam between the layers.
7. Garnish the top of the cake with fresh raspberries.

INGREDIENTS

- *1/4 cup almond flour**
- *1/4 cup coconut flour**
- *1/4 cup unsweetened applesauce*
- *2 eggs*
- *1/4 cup almond milk*
- *1 teaspoon baking powder*
- *1/2 teaspoon vanilla extract*
- *Sugar-free raspberry chia jam for filling*
- *Fresh raspberries for garnish*

Using the measurements above will make exactly one serving of this meal. This serving size will match the nutritional information on this page.

Healthy Highlights:

WHOLE GRAIN | HEALTHY FATS | LEAN PROTEIN

* This recipe contains a healthy highlight that we don't recommend you switch with other ingredients

124

Treacle Tart with Almond Crust

NUTRITION INFORMATION

- *Calories: 290*
- *Carbohydrates: 30g*
- *Protein: 7g*
- *Fats: 16g*
- *Sugar: 8g*
- *Sodium: 200mg*

DIRECTIONS:

1. Preheat the air fryer to 160°C (320°F) for 3 minutes.
2. In a bowl, mix almond flour, shredded coconut, melted butter, sugar-free golden syrup or molasses, egg, vanilla extract, and a pinch of salt until well combined.
3. Press the mixture into a small greased tart tin or ramekin to form the crust.
4. Place the tart tin in the air fryer basket.
5. Cook for 15-18 minutes until the crust is golden and firm.
6. Let the crust cool completely before filling with your favourite treacle tart filling or topping.

INGREDIENTS

- *1/2 cup almond flour**
- *1/4 cup unsweetened shredded coconut*
- *1/4 cup butter, melted*
- *2 tablespoons sugar-free golden syrup or molasses*
- *1 egg*
- *1/2 teaspoon vanilla extract*
- *Pinch of salt*

Using the measurements above will make exactly one serving of this meal. This serving size will match the nutritional information on this page.

Healthy Highlights:

WHOLE GRAIN | HEALTHY FATS | LEAN PROTEIN

* This recipe contains a healthy highlight that we don't recommend you switch with other ingredients

Lemon Chia Seed Cake with Stevia Glaze

NUTRITION INFORMATION

- *Calories: 250*
- *Carbohydrates: 20g*
- *Protein: 5g*
- *Fats: 16g*
- *Sugar: 5g*
- *Sodium: 150mg*

DIRECTIONS:

1. Preheat the air fryer to 160°C (320°F) for 3 minutes.
2. In a mixing bowl, combine almond flour, coconut flour, unsweetened almond milk, melted coconut oil, lemon juice, chia seeds, egg, baking powder, and lemon zest. Mix until smooth.
3. Pour the batter into a greased small cake tin or ramekin.
4. Place the cake tin in the air fryer basket.
5. Cook for 20-25 minutes until the cake is golden and a toothpick inserted into the centre comes out clean.
6. Let the cake cool slightly before drizzling with sugar-free stevia glaze.

INGREDIENTS

- 1/4 cup almond flour*
- 1/4 cup coconut flour*
- 1/4 cup unsweetened almond milk
- 2 tablespoons coconut oil, melted
- 2 tablespoons lemon juice
- 1 tablespoon chia seeds
- 1 egg
- 1/2 teaspoon baking powder
- 1/4 teaspoon lemon zest
- Sugar-free stevia glaze for topping

Using the measurements above will make exactly one serving of this meal. This serving size will match the nutritional information on this page.

Healthy Highlights:

WHOLE GRAIN | HEALTHY FATS | LEAN PROTEIN

* This recipe contains a healthy highlight that we don't recommend you switch with other ingredients

Scones with Sugar-Free Clotted Cream and Berry Compote

NUTRITION INFORMATION

- Calories: 220
- Carbohydrates: 20g
- Protein: 5g
- Fats: 14g
- Sugar: 5g
- Sodium: 150mg

DIRECTIONS:

1. Preheat the air fryer to 160°C (320°F) for 3 minutes.
2. In a mixing bowl, combine almond flour, coconut flour, unsweetened almond milk, melted coconut oil, egg, sugar-free sweetener, baking powder, and a pinch of salt. Mix until a dough forms.
3. Divide the dough into small portions and shape into scones.
4. Place the scones on a greased air fryer tray or basket.
5. Cook for 15-18 minutes until the scones are golden and cooked through.
6. While the scones are cooking, prepare the clotted cream by mixing Greek yogurt, whipped coconut cream, vanilla extract, and sugar-free sweetener in a bowl.
7. For the berry compote, simmer mixed berries with water and sugar-free sweetener in a saucepan until thickened.
8. Serve the warm scones with sugar-free clotted cream and berry compote.

*This recipe contains a healthy highlight that we don't recommend you switch with other ingredients

INGREDIENTS

- 1/2 cup almond flour*
- 1/4 cup coconut flour*
- 1/4 cup unsweetened almond milk
- 2 tablespoons coconut oil, melted
- 1 egg
- 1 tablespoon sugar-free sweetener
- 1/2 teaspoon baking powder
- Pinch of salt
- 1/4 cup Greek yogurt

- 1/4 cup sugar-free coconut cream
- 1 teaspoon vanilla extract
- Sugar-free sweetener to taste

- 1/2 cup mixed berries (fresh or frozen)
- 1 tablespoon water
- Sugar-free sweetener to taste

Using the measurements above will make exactly one serving of this meal. This serving size will match the nutritional information on this page.

Healthy Highlights:

- WHOLE GRAIN
- HEALTHY FATS
- LEAN PROTEIN

Sugar-Free Bread and Butter Pudding with Coconut Cream

NUTRITION INFORMATION

- *Calories: 280*
- *Carbohydrates: 25g*
- *Protein: 6g*
- *Fats: 18g*
- *Sugar: 5g*
- *Sodium: 200mg*

DIRECTIONS:

1. Preheat the air fryer to 160°C (320°F) for 3 minutes.
2. In a bowl, whisk together egg, almond milk, melted coconut oil, sugar-free sweetener, vanilla extract, and cinnamon.
3. Add the toasted bread cubes to the egg mixture and let them soak for a few minutes.
4. Transfer the bread mixture to a small greased baking dish or ramekin.
5. Place the baking dish in the air fryer basket.
6. Cook for 15-18 minutes until the bread pudding is set and golden.
7. Serve warm with sugar-free coconut cream.

INGREDIENTS

- 2 slices low-carb bread, toasted and cut into cubes
- 1 egg
- 1/4 cup unsweetened almond milk*
- 1 tablespoon coconut oil, melted
- 1 tablespoon sugar-free sweetener
- 1/2 teaspoon vanilla extract
- Pinch of cinnamon
- Sugar-free coconut cream for serving

Using the measurements above will make exactly one serving of this meal. This serving size will match the nutritional information on this page.

Healthy Highlights:

WHOLE GRAIN | HEALTHY FATS | LEAN PROTEIN

* This recipe contains a healthy highlight that we don't recommend you switch with other ingredients

Rhubarb Crumble with Almond Flour Topping

NUTRITION INFORMATION

- Calories: 250
- Carbohydrates: 20g
- Protein: 5g
- Fats: 16g
- Sugar: 8g
- Sodium: 200mg

DIRECTIONS:

1. Preheat the air fryer to 160°C (320°F) for 3 minutes.
2. In a bowl, toss chopped rhubarb with sugar-free sweetener and water.
3. In another bowl, mix almond flour, chopped almonds, melted coconut oil, sugar-free sweetener, and cinnamon to make the crumble topping.
4. Place the rhubarb mixture in a small greased baking dish or ramekin.
5. Sprinkle the crumble topping evenly over the rhubarb.
6. Place the baking dish in the air fryer basket.
7. Cook for 15-18 minutes until the topping is golden and the rhubarb is tender.
8. Serve warm as a delicious dessert.

*This recipe contains a healthy highlight that we don't recommend you switch with other ingredients

INGREDIENTS

- 1 cup chopped rhubarb
- 1 tablespoon sugar-free sweetener
- 1 tablespoon water

- 1/2 cup almond flour*
- 1/4 cup chopped almonds
- 2 tablespoons coconut oil, melted
- 1 tablespoon sugar-free sweetener
- Pinch of cinnamon

Using the measurements above will make exactly one serving of this meal. This serving size will match the nutritional information on this page.

Healthy Highlights:

WHOLE GRAIN | HEALTHY FATS | LEAN PROTEIN

Conclusion

WE'RE THRILLED IF YOU'VE ENJOYED OUR COOKBOOK

We appreciate you choosing this cookbook and hope it's been a valuable resource in your kitchen adventures. We're thrilled if you've enjoyed whipping up tasty meals with your trusty airfryer while keeping your blood sugar levels in check. Here's to many more culinary delights and good health ahead!

As you explore outside of the recipes of our cookbook, we hope you'll keep following our handy portion control tips. We really suggest sticking with the ingredients we recommend for each recipe, but if you're feeling adventurous, go ahead and try some new twists! Just remember to keep those whole grains, healthy fats, and lean proteins front and centre in your meals. They're absolute gems for managing diabetes, so it's best to steer clear of less nutritious options.

Your body will definitely appreciate the extra care, and we're cheering for a healthier you!

And hey, if you've found this cookbook helpful, why not explore more books in our collection? Whether you're seeking more recipes, tips on cooking for other dietary needs or ways to live healthier, there's a whole world of knowledge waiting for you. Keep cooking, keep exploring, and keep prioritising your well-being. Cheers to good eats and good health!

Printed in Great Britain
by Amazon